D0170136

ODDBALL INDIANA

A Guide to Some Really
STRANGE PLACES

JEROME POHLEN

CHICAGO
REVIEW
PRESS

Library of Congress Cataloging-in-Publication Data

Pohlen, Jerome.
   Oddball Indiana : a guide to some really strange places / Jerome Pohlen.
      p. cm.
   Includes bibliographical references and indexes.
   ISBN 1-55652-438-2
      1. Indiana —Guidebooks. 2. Indiana—History, Local—Miscellanea.
   3. Curiosities and wonders—Indiana. I. Title.
   F524.3 .P64 2002
   917.7204'44—dc21

                                                      2001052476

The author has made every effort to secure permissions for all the material in this book.
If any acknowledgment has inadvertently been omitted, please contact the author.

All photographs courtesy of Jerome Pohlen unless otherwise noted.
Cover and interior design: Mel Kupfer

Published by Chicago Review Press, Incorporated
814 North Franklin Street
Chicago, Illinois 60610
ISBN 1-55652-438-2
Printed in the United States of America
5 4 3 2

TO JOEY, ZAK, MATTHEW,
SAMANTHA, ERIC, DANIEL,
AND MILO.

Contents

INtroDuCtioN ix

1. NortHerN INDiaNa 1
Map of Northern Indiana 54–55

2. CeNtral INDiaNa 57
Map of Central Indiana 108–109

3. SoUtHerN INDiaNa 111
Map of Southern Indiana 166–167

4. INDiaNaPoLiS Area 169

5. DiLLiNGer'S DiaPerS-to-DeatH toUr 191

EPiLoGUe 205

ACkNoWLeDGMeNtS 207

ReCoMMeNDeD SoUrCeS 209

INDeX BY CitY NaMe 215

INDeX BY Site NaMe 223

INTRODUCTION

*Q*uick—what do these things have in common: Ben Hur, the birthplace of the automobile, Oscar the Monster Turtle, the World's Largest Egg, Johnny Appleseed's grave, and the Kinsey Institute for Research in Sex, Gender, and Reproduction? Drawing a blank? What about the invention of the pay toilet, Hollywood's first Tarzan, the original People's Temple, and the World's Largest Stump? Still without a clue? How about the birth-places of corn flakes, Dan Quayle, square donuts, and Wonder Bread? That's right—they're all in Indiana!

While other travel guides tell you about yet another oh-so-quaint bed-and-breakfast, one more bike trail through Brown County, or that small-town diner where you can waste away the day with a bottomless cup of coffee while chatting with Flo, *Oddball Indiana* gives you the information you *really* need. What happened when the good folk of Plainfield decided to dump a former President of the United States into a mud puddle? Why is Nancy Barnett's grave in the middle of a county road? How did David Letterman get fired from his first broadcasting gig? Who invented Alka-Seltzer? And where can you go to contact your dead Aunt Clara? These are the Indiana questions people want answered. Or at least weird people. People like you.

And there's no excuse for not hitting the Hoosier highways in search of the strange. It's the smallest state west of the Appalachians (except Hawaii), and, what's more, it's the "Crossroads of the Nation." Seven interstate highways pass through its borders, more than any other state: I-64, I-65, I-69, I-70, I-80/90, I-74, and I-465. Plenty of roads and odd things to see . . . what are you waiting for? You should be laughing on your vacation, not lounging. Get moving!

But first, a little advice. In this book, I've tried to give clear directions from major streets and landmarks, but you could still make a wrong turn. Don't panic, and remember these Oddball travel tips:

• Stop and ask! For a lot of communities, their Oddball attraction might be their only claim to fame. Locals are often thrilled that you'd drive out of your way to marvel at their underappreciated shrine. But choose your guides wisely; old cranks at the town café are good for information; pimply teenage clerks at the 7-Eleven are not.

• Call ahead. Few Oddball sites keep regular hours, but most will gladly wait around if they know you're coming. Some Indiana sites are seasonal, or can close at a moment's notice if the proprietor needs to run an errand. Always call.

• Don't give up. Think of that little old lady who's volunteered her days to keep that small town museum open; she's waiting just for you. She's not standing out on the corner, hollering at passersby— you have to find her. That's *your* job.

• Don't trespass! Don't become a Terrible Tourist. Just because somebody erected a gigantic monument to a peach doesn't mean you're invited to crawl all over it.

• Persevere: Road-tripping is hard work. If you find yourself out of sorts after hours in the car, remember these Indiana folk cures: for arthritis of the fingers, catch and strangle a weasel barehanded; for a stuffed-up head, sniff a dirty sock nine times; and for stammering, a smart slap is the face with raw liver should do the trick.

Do you have an Oddball site of your own? Have I missed anything? Do you know of an Oddball site that should be included in a later version? Please write and let me know: Chicago Review Press, 814 North Franklin Street, Chicago, Illinois 60610.

Northern Indiana

*I*f all you know about Northern Indiana is the toll from East Chicago to Angola, perhaps you should slow down. And while you're at it, show a little respect. First of all, if it wasn't for this admittedly flat and corn-covered region, your vacation might be a whole lot less enjoyable—these folks practically *invented* the Great American Road Trip. The prairie schooner wagon, probably the first long-distance "family car," was manufactured for pioneers by the Studebaker family of South Bend. Road technology was perfected on the coast-to-coast Lincoln Highway, which still bisects the region. And today, most of this nation's recreational vehicles and motor homes are manufactured in and around Elkhart. When you're touring the back roads of Shipshewana, Winamac, and Napanee, you're driving on hallowed ground.

And not just hallowed ground, but *strange* ground. Look around. Where else can you find a 3,000-pound egg, a skinny-dipping ghost, Munchkin handprints in cement, and Oscar the Monster Turtle? Where will you find the birthplaces of Alka-Seltzer, heavier-than-air flight, and Michael Jackson? And where can you find the remains of Johnny Appleseed and the World's First Ferris Wheel? Nowhere in the world but the top third of the Hoosier State, that's where.

Angola
Lottery Bowl

Hold on, compulsive gamblers! The Lottery Bowl isn't a new scratch-and-win game from the Indiana legislature. No, in this lottery you play for your life.

Resting in a simple cabinet on the top floor of Tri-State University's athletic facility is one of the Selective Service System's most recognizable artifacts: the Lottery Bowl. This two-foot-tall goldfish tank was purchased from a Washington, D.C., pet store at the outset of World War I. It was used to select numbers that translated into draft notices to thousands of young American men from 1917 to 1918. Following the Armistice, the draft ended and the glass bowl was mothballed in Philadelphia.

Just before the United States' entry into World War II, President Roosevelt sent a limousine to pick up the Lottery Bowl and escort it to the nation's capital. The Selective Service was reinstituted in 1940 and continued farming young men through 1970. For all but one of those years it operated under the direction of General Lewis B. Hershey, Tri-State graduate and namesake of this college's gym.

Several of Hershey's personal effects (such as his ceremonial saber) are also on display at Hershey Hall, as are other items from the history of the Selective Service—but it's the Lottery Bowl that draws the visitors. How ironic to find it just up the road from the hometown of Dan Quayle, one of history's most dubious draft avoiders.

Hershey Hall, Tri-State University, 1 University Ave., Angola, IN 46703

(260) 665-4100 or (260) 665-4141

Hours: Most days; call ahead

Cost: Free

www.tristate.edu/Athletics/sub_facilities.html

Directions: South of Rte. 20 (Maumee St.), just west of the railroad tracks at the end of Park St.

Auburn
Auburn Cord Duesenberg Museum

When you first step into this impressive museum, you'll know you've found "a duesy," and not just one, but more than a hundred.

The life of the Auburn Cord Duesenberg company was short but brilliant. Started by the Eckhart family in 1902, it closed in 1937. Its most remarkable models were created after E. L. Cord was hired as the company's president in 1924. The top-of-the-line Duesenbergs he designed embodied the spirit of the Roaring Twenties, with Art Deco interiors and powerful engines—why else would they be named Speedsters? These babies could max out at 130 MPH and were the cars of choice for screen stars such as Clark Gable and Gary Cooper.

You'll see more of these classic autos here, in the company's restored 1930 corporate headquarters, than anywhere else. All are in mint condition, yet nobody would think of driving them at 130 MPH anymore. The Model J, introduced in 1929, was the make's most popular high-end model; each vehicle had a unique body and was driven 500 miles on the Indianapolis Motor Speedway before delivery. At the time, the Model J had double the horsepower of every other car on the road.

The museum's six galleries feature the entire Auburn Cord Duesenberg line, as well as other Indiana-manufactured autos, like the homely 1952 Crosley. Each Labor Day the town throws an Auburn Cord Duesenberg Festival, capped off by a car auction. This isn't a repo sale at the auto pound—some of the cars sold here are worth more than $1 million.

1600 S. Wayne St., PO Box 271, Auburn, IN 46706-0271

(260) 925-1444

Hours: Daily 9 A.M.–5 P.M.

Cost: Adults $7, Seniors $6, Kids $4.50

www.acdmuseum.org

ACD Festival: www.acdfestival.org

Directions: South on Jackson St. from Rte. 8 until it bends westward, intersecting with Wayne St.

Beverly Shores
The House of Tomorrow

At the end of the 1934 Chicago "Century of Progress" World's Fair, organizers sold off most of the exhibits to the highest bidders. Several of the exhibition's futuristic model homes ended up across Lake Michigan in Beverly Shores, where folks were anxious for progress.

The House of Tomorrow, a 12-sided home with more windows than walls, still towers above its fellow Fair refugees on Lake Front Drive.

Across the street, clinging to the shoreline, the pink stucco Florida Tropical House looks as if it would be more at home in Miami Beach. All the adjacent Cypress House needs, with its swampy cypress shingles and siding, is a fan boat and some alligator traps. Two additional buildings demonstrated futuristic building technologies that are now part of the past: the Rostone House was manufactured with synthetic cast stone, the Armco Ferro House with prefab steel.

Still, not everyone in Beverly Shores was interested in things to come back in the 1930s; some liked the way things were a century and a half earlier. Another developer brought six replicas of historic buildings to this dunes community: Wakefield House (the birthplace of George Washington), Boston's Old North Church, Mount Vernon, the Paul Revere House, Longfellow's Wayside Inn, and the House of Seven Gables. Only the Old North Church remains, converted to a private residence. The rest have been torn down, or burned down.

Lake Front Dr., Beverly Shores, IN 46301

(219) 926-7561

Hours: Always visible

Cost: Free

Directions: Between E. State Park Rd. and Broadway, on Lake Front Dr.

Old North Church, Eaton Ave. & Beverly Dr., Beverly Shores, IN 46301

Private phone

Hours: Always visible

Cost: Free

Directions: One block west of Broadway on Beverly Dr.

Bremen
World's Fattest Man Death Site

Robert Earl Hughes was touring with the Gooding Brothers Amusement Company in the summer of 1958 when he came down with a case of the measles. For most people, this would have been a minor difficulty, but for the World's Fattest Man, it was serious.

Hughes's 1,041-pound body (he once tipped the scales at 1,069) could not fit through the doors of the Bremen Community Hospital, so doctors were forced to treat Hughes in his customized trailer in the parking lot. The 32-year-old sideshow performer was just getting over the disease when he contracted uremia and died soon thereafter, on July 10, 1958. Several days later he was laid to rest in a piano-sized coffin in his hometown, Mt. Sterling, Illinois.

Little of the Bremen Community Hospital of 1958 remains, but several of the current interior rooms are the same ones Hughes was unable to fit into. A new facility has been expanded on the site with, presumably, wider doors.

Bremen Community Hospital, PO Box 8, 411 S. Whitlock St., Bremen, IN 46506

(574) 546-2211

Hours: Always visible

Cost: Free

Directions: Three blocks south of Rte. 106/331, five blocks east of the Rte. 331 intersection.

Chesterton
Diana of the Dunes

Indiana's best-known ghost is also a nudist, much to the delight of folks visiting Indiana Dunes State Park. She has been named Diana of the Dunes, but in real life she was Alice Mable Gray.

Gray hailed from Chicago, the daughter of a prominent Illinois physician and a graduate of the University of Chicago. Forsaking her inheritance for a simpler life, she moved into a shack (dubbed Driftwood) on the shore of Lake Michigan in 1915. There she would spend long days strolling on the beach and skinny-dipping in the icy waters.

Alice met a drifter and ex-con named Paul Wilson, and the two were married in 1921. They produced a daughter, Bonita. Paul was often absent, usually running from the law. He was accused in 1922 of murdering a vagrant and burning the body near Alice's shack, but was never formally charged with the crime.

While the dunes are picturesque, they're not exactly conducive to healthy living—particularly if you live in a shack. Poor Alice wasted away, eventually dying of uremic poisoning on the night of February 8–9, 1925, following the birth of her second child. Some think her demise was brought on by injuries suffered at the hands of Paul Wilson. Once again, allegations could not be substantiated. Gray was buried in Gary in a pauper's grave in Oak Hill Cemetery, but her soul remained on the shores of her beloved lake.

Rangers and visitors still see her emerge, naked, from the waters throughout the year. Before she can be detained for indecent exposure, she vanishes. If you're female and a practicing nudist, you can use this legend to your advantage.

Indiana Dunes State Park, 1600 N. Rte. 25 East, Chesterton, IN 46304

(219) 926-1952

Hours: Daily, dawn–dusk

Cost: In-state, $3; Out-of-state, $5

www.duneland.com

www.state.in.us/dnr/parklake/parks/indianadunes.html

Directions: At the north end of Rte. 49.

Historical Society of Ogden Dunes, 8 Lupine Lane, Ogden Dunes, IN 46368

No phone

E-mail: youngmanpe@yahoo.com

Hours: By appointment, via e-mail

Cost: Donations accepted

members.tripod.com/~Ogden_Dunes/index.html

Directions: Two blocks south of Shore Dr. off Hillcrest Rd.

BENTON
A 10-foot-tall headless ghost of a murdered miser has long been spotted by passing motorists near the graveyard on Rte. 33 north of Benton. Some drivers are chased by the spirit, who often wields a club.

BLUFFTON
Two interurban trains, one empty, one full, collided north of Bluffton on September 21, 1910, killing 41 passengers.

DECATUR
Each Halloween, Decatur throws a Callithumpian Parade. The deliberately noisy parade was started in 1926 and was aimed to scare kids away from getting into mischief.

Don't let this frighten you away.

The Oz Museum

When the Yellow Brick Road Gift Shop opened in 1979, its name was more or less pulled out of a hat. But what started as a typical collectibles store turned into an Oz obsession for owner Jean Nelson. She began contacting individuals who had been associated with the 1939 movie, many of whom had played Munchkins. In 1982, Chesterton celebrated its first Oz Festival, and has been hosting it ever since.

With so many props left over from the festivals, the Yellow Brick Road Gift Shop opened a one-room museum in the back of the store. It's filled with memorabilia, Oz fan artwork, and re-created movie artifacts like the Wicked Witch of the West's hourglass, Dorothy's gingham dress, and (of course!) the ruby slippers. A long diorama showing Dorothy's journey through Oz lines one wall of the museum. On the left she's crushing one witch with her house and on the right she's melting another, before heading back to Kansas. The year it was dedicated, actress Margaret Hamilton spent several days at the shop, proving to visitors she was hardly as frightening without the green makeup and the flying monkeys. Along another wall is a group of smiling, robotic characters who rock back and forth in unison. Outside, a dozen Munchkin handprints are pressed into cement.

Nelson sold her shop in 2001, but new owners Marilyn Zengler, Linda Spry, and Gerard Bishop keep the spirit alive. Chesterton continues to host the Oz Festival on the third weekend in September every year. Surviving Munchkins are always invited, but sadly, only a few are left on this side of the rainbow.

109 E. Yellow Brick Rd. (County Road 950N), Chesterton, IN 46304

(219) 926-7048

E-mail: yellowbrickrdshop@yahoo.com

Hours: Tuesday–Saturday 10 A.M.–5 P.M., Sunday 11 A.M.–4 P.M.

Cost: 25¢

www.yellowbrickroadonline.com

Wizard of Oz Festival: www.cebunet.com/oz/

Directions: Just south of the Indiana Toll Road (I-80/90) off Rte. 49.

Churubusco
Oscar, the Beast of 'Busco

In 1948, ducks and fish began mysteriously disappearing from farmer Gale Harris's small lake northwest of Churubusco. A rumor began circulating that a pickup-sized snapping turtle was to blame. Local residents organized a turtle hunt in 1949 to snare the beast they'd named Oscar. After several fruitless days and nights searching Fulk Lake, the often-drunken posse abandoned hope of capturing the 400-pound quacker-killer. But not Harris.

Like Captain Ahab, Gale Harris never gave up his quest for his shelled nemesis. One night he was able to wrap a chain around the creature, which he then hitched to four workhorses. An epic tug-of-war ensued, and the chain was the loser. It snapped, and Oscar dove for the lake's bottom.

A turtle strong enough to overpower four horses? Certainly it was no average duck-devouring reptile, but the very Beast of 'Busco! Though the renamed monster was never seen again, there's no guarantee it's not still lurking in the mud, waiting for its next meal. Churubusco calls itself "Turtle City, USA" to this day, has a statue to Oscar in the community park, and celebrates Turtle Days every June.

Fulk Lake, Madden Rd., Churubusco, IN 46723

No phone

Hours: Always visible

Cost: Free

Directions: Head northeast 2 miles on Rte. 205, turn left on Madden Rd., head north 1
  mile to the pond just south of County Line Rd.

Spinning wheels don't always go 'round.

Dunns Bridge
Remains of the World's First Ferris Wheel

The World's First Ferris Wheel was constructed for Chicago's 1893 Columbian Exposition, yet parts of it have outlived everyone who ever rode it above the Midway. How? Following the suspiciously convenient fires during the closing days of the Exposition, the Ferris wheel was disassembled and rebuilt on the north side of Chicago. Operating there, it thrilled riders for several years before being carted to Missouri for the 1904 St. Louis World's Fair.

After its second appearance at a World Exposition, the wheel was sold off in pieces for iron scrap. One buyer was Indiana farmer Isaac Dunn. He wanted to connect two pieces of land that straddled the Kankakee River west of North Judson, and welded several pieces of the old ride together to accomplish the task. Exactly which pieces of the wheel he bought are up for debate, but this much is clear to the novice observer: this thing sure didn't start out as a bridge.

A tiny burg eventually grew up around the unique structure, and locals dubbed their town Dunns Bridge. A new bridge spans the water today, but what's left of the World's First Ferris Wheel, newly repainted, still arcs the river just west of the road.

County Road 400E, Dunns Bridge, IN 46392

No phone

Hours: Always visible

Cost: Free

Directions: Off Rte. 10 east of Wheatfield, north two miles on County Road 400E
  (Tefft Rd.) to the Kankakee River.

Dyer
The "Ideal Section" and the Ostermann Bench

If you've ever wondered, while sitting in bumper-to-bumper traffic on an ugly interstate, searching desperately for a rest stop, whether anyone has ever tried to build a better highway, the answer is yes—80 years ago! When this nation began its love affair with the automobile, a few visionaries realized that road construction technology would have to keep pace with faster and more numerous cars. This need was made all the more clear when Henry Ostermann, an early booster of the Lincoln Highway, hit a slippery shoulder near Tama, Iowa, on June 7, 1920. His Studebaker spun out of control, overturned, and killed the auto dealer.

Ostermann's friends used the tragedy to convince U.S. Rubber to fund an experiment on a two-mile stretch of Route 30 in Dyer, Indiana.

The initial plans for the so-called Ideal Section of the Lincoln Highway were, to say the least, impressive. Wide shoulders. Banked curves with proper drainage. Sidewalks and street lights. Landscaped rest stops and free campsites!

But the reality of the Ideal Section didn't match up with the plan. To start with, the original 2-mile stretch was shortened to 1.3 miles after an adjacent cranky farmer named Moeller refused to sell his right-of-way, opting to hold out for more money.

The project began in 1921, but it would be two years before it was completed. Engineers were flying blind, and the frustration showed. The head contractor for the Ideal Section's only bridge, Fred Tapp, committed suicide on October 5, 1922, in a manner only a contractor might choose: he blew himself up with a stick of dynamite clutched against his chest. The rest stops were never built. Farmer Moeller eventually sold part of his land for campsites but they, too, were never constructed. A local energy company agreed to power the streetlights for free, but pulled the plug after a year. Nearby residents walked off with plants used for land-scaping, the sidewalks were eventually ripped out, and Fred Tapp's bridge was replaced.

All that remains of the Ideal Section is a memorial bench to Henry Ostermann. To get to this humble stone monument, you have to stumble along the weed-choked shoulder—conspicuously free of sidewalks and streetlights—just feet from traffic on a less-than-ideal highway.

Rte. 30 & St. John's Rd., Dyer, IN 46311

No phone

Hours: Always visible

Cost: Free

www.lincolnhighwayassoc.org/info/in/

Directions: Just west of Meyer's Castle (1370 Joliet St.) on Rte. 30, on the south side of the highway.

ELKHART
Barbers cannot threaten to cut off youngsters' ears in Elkhart.

Why don't you go play on the sidewalk?!?!!

East Chicago
Park on the Sidewalk, Walk in the Street

Has the whole world gone topsy-turvy? In East Chicago it has, at least in the neighborhood of Marktown. This poorly conceived, company-built community has streets that are so narrow residents must park their cars on the sidewalks. With all the cars on the walkways, everyone strolls in the streets. When parents in Marktown tell their children, "Go play in the street!" they mean it!

The homes in Marktown have a strangely European appearance, tight and communal. If you added a few canals you'd think you were in a run-down Dutch village. This 15-block community is shoehorned between a steel plant and a refinery, well off the beaten track, yet still only minutes from Chicago.

Riley & Dickey Rds., East Chicago, IN 46312

No phone

Hours: Always visible

Cost: Free

Directions: Neighborhood bound by 129th St., Dickey Rd., Pine St., and Riley Rd.; exit Riley Rd. from Cline Ave. and head northeast.

Elkhart Birthplace of Alka-Seltzer

Sunday morning in Elkhart.

Plop, plop, fizz, fizz, oh what a relief it is . . . but it almost wasn't. Were it not for an editor who fancied himself a doctor and a businessman who fancied himself an investigator, Alka-Seltzer might not exist today.

During the late 1920s, the nation was gripped with one flu epidemic after another. But strangely enough, reporters, editors, and typesetters at the *Elkhart Truth* seemed to be resistant to the nasty bugs. Andrew "Hub" Beardsley, president of Elkhart's Dr. Miles Medical Company, was paying a visit to the local paper and asked the editor in chief why everyone was at work. It was the editor's concoction of aspirin and baking soda that did the trick—everyone on staff took it!

Beardsley recognized the medicine's potential and asked one of his chemists, Maurice Treneer, to make it more appealing to the public. Treneer mixed the two ingredients into an effervescent tablet, and Alka-Seltzer was born. That's right, the fizz is just a marketing gimmick.

Alka-Seltzer hit the shelves in 1931. The Dr. Miles Medical Company (now Miles Laboratories, a division of Bayer AG) is also responsible for inventing One-A-Day multivitamins and Flintstone and Bugs Bunny chewable vitamins.

421 S. Second St., Elkhart, IN 46516
(574) 294-1661
Hours: Always visible
Cost: Free
www.alkaseltzer.com
Directions: At the corner of Franklin St. and Second St. (Rte. 19).

Curly Top and the Toothpick Train

Railroad museums are a dime a dozen. It's not as if you can throw a loco-motive in the trash. Park it in an old switching yard—voilà—instant museum! But the National New York Central is not a typical railroad museum because of two special exhibits. The first is a collection of auto-graphs, and the second is the Toothpick Train.

During the Depression, a local girl named Violet Schmidt had a unique hobby. Each day she would wait out beside the New York Central tracks and wave to the passengers headed someplace more interesting, like Chicago or New York. Because the Twentieth Century Limited moved so fast ("960 miles in 960 minutes"), riders could only recognize Schmidt by her most prominent characteristic: her curly hair. It soon became a custom for riders to reward the loyal Curly Top by tossing her auto-graphed menus, or, for those with a better pitching arm, notes hidden in hollowed potatoes. Whether or not they were trying to bean her, Schmidt saved the best-known autographs, including Al Jolson, Shirley Temple, Spencer Tracy, and President Herbert Hoover. You can see them at the museum today.

Another amazing exhibit at this museum was a lifelong project from an obsessed New York Central fan. Terry Woodlings used 421,250 tooth-picks and a lot of glue to build a replica of an early steam locomotive on the NYC line. Woodlings's elaborate model is encased in glass, lest a visitor with a popcorn kernel stuck between a couple of molars try to make it a 421,249-toothpick train.

National New York Central Museum, 721 S. Main St., PO Box 1708, Elkhart, IN 46515
(574) 294-3001
E-mail: artscul@elkhartindiana.org
Hours: Tuesday–Friday 10 A.M.–2 P.M., Saturday 10 A.M.–4 P.M., Sunday noon–4 P.M.
Cost: Adults $2, Seniors (62+) $1, Kids (6–12) $1

Directions: At the south end of downtown, where Main St. crosses the railroad tracks.

"You can't take sex, booze, or weekends away from the American people." —John K. Hanson
Photo by author, courtesy of RV/MH Heritage Foundation

RV/MH Heritage Foundation/Hall of Fame

If road-tripping were a religion, Elkhart would be Mecca. Most of this nation's recreational vehicles and conversion vans are, and always have been, built in and around this northern Indiana city. It's also the location of the RV/MH Heritage Foundation, the repository of all manufacturing information pertaining to recreational vehicles (RVs) and motor homes (MHs), from their 1930s genesis to the present.

More than 20 restored recreational vehicles circle fake campfires in this shedlike building. Flat cutouts of 1950s families roast cardboard weenies and commune with nature, American style. Most of the vehicles are open, so you can step inside to check out the amenities and period decorations. The collection includes the World's First Winnebago, a 1967 model, and a 28-foot 1940 New Moon, the model Lucille Ball and Desi Arnaz pulled across the country in *The Long, Long Trailer*. Though it looked big onscreen, it barely compares to another model on display, the 1954 Spartan Imperial. This 8-foot-wide, 41-foot-long behemoth has a master bedroom, a full bath, two children's bunk beds, a kitchen with a pantry, and a nice-sized living room.

For true RV/MH nuts, visit the foundation's library to learn how to restore your Airstream, Fan Luxury Liner, or Magic Carpet Pop-Up. This wonderful resource center is doing its part to preserve part of the sentiments once expressed by Winnebago founder John K. Hanson: "You can't take sex, booze, or weekends away from the American people." Thank God!

801 Benham Ave., Elkhart, IN 46516

(800) 378-8694 or (574) 293-2344

E-mail: RVMHHALL@aol.com

Hours: Monday–Friday 9 A.M.–4 P.M.; weekends by appointment

Cost: Adults $3

www.rv-mh-hall-of-fame.org

Directions: Just south of downtown, south of the railroad tracks, on Rte. 19 (Benham Ave.).

Fort Wayne
"Fish Eaters and Idol Worshipers"

There was a time, not too long ago, when anti-Catholic sentiment ran fairly close to the surface in the American psyche. The prejudice was not limited to hate-mongering groups like the Ku Klux Klan or the John Birch Society, as you will see if you visit a collection compiled by John Francis Noll, the fifth bishop of Fort Wayne, at the Cathedral Museum.

Take the bishop-bashing cartoons that appeared in *Harper's Weekly*. One 1871 drawing by Thomas Nast shows bishops crawling out of the "American River Ganges," their crocodile-toothed miters open to devour American schoolchildren. (You might know Nast as the artist who created the modern, white-bearded, jelly-bellied image of Santa, and the elephant as the mascot of the Republican Party.) And there's more, including books, caricatures, and modern religious tracts you might be handed on a street corner to this day.

The Cathedral Museum also has a large collection of items related to the local diocese, a full-size statue of the very small Pope Pius X, nun dolls dressed in dozens of religious orders' vestments, and two splinters from the cross on which Jesus was crucified . . . or so the sign says.

Cathedral Museum, S. Calhoun & E. Lewis Sts., Fort Wayne, IN 46802

(260) 424-1485

Hours: Wednesday–Friday 10 A.M.–2 P.M., 2nd and 4th Sundays, Noon–3 P.M.

Cost: Free

Directions: One block west of the southbound stretch of Rte. 27, downtown.

The last appleseed to be planted.

Johnny Appleseed's Grave

John Chapman was America's first hippie. Better known as Johnny Appleseed, he was looked upon with some suspicion by many he met. Maybe it
was his claim that God had commanded him in a dream to plant apple
trees along the western migration. Maybe it was his devotion to the Swe-
denborgian faith, passing out Bibles as often as tree saplings. Most likely,
it was the tin pot he wore for a hat, or that he made drinking water in the
winter by melting snow with his dirty feet.

During his travels, Chapman covered a region of 100,000 square miles, starting nurseries from New England to the Midwest. On a trip to Fort Wayne in March 1845, he contracted pneumonia after walking barefoot through the snow to visit an apple orchard. This would have been a stupid act for a young man, but he was 72 years old at the time. He never made it to 73. He died on March 18, 1845.

Chapman was buried in the Archer family plot, located roughly where the city's power lines run along the river today. His exact burial spot is unknown, but there is a gravestone atop a small hill in the center of a park named after him. For all anyone knows, footings for the transmission towers could have been drilled through his remains.

Fort Wayne celebrates Johnny Appleseed with a festival each September.

Johnny Appleseed Memorial Park, 4000 block of Parnell Ave., Fort Wayne, IN 46802
No phone
Hours: Always visible
Cost: Free
www.msc.cornell.edu/~weeds/SchoolPages/Appleseed/welcome.html
Directions: Just south of Rte. 14 and War Memorial Coliseum, in the former
   City Utilities Park.

THANKS A LOT, JOHNNY!
Chapman didn't spread just apples across our new nation, but also a plant called dog fennel. He thought the noxious weed cured fevers, so he scattered dog fennel seeds *everywhere*. Today, this botanical nuisance is sometimes referred to as "Johnnyweed."

Lincoln Museum

Abraham Lincoln never had much to do with the city of Fort Wayne, but the town is the headquarters of Lincoln National Life Insurance. This corporation has amassed a collection of over 18,000 artifacts from the life and legacy of the Great Emancipator, one of the largest in the nation. It is all on display in a new interactive museum.

They have the inkwell used to sign the Emancipation Proclamation, the photo used as the model for the $5 bill, the flag from Abe's box at Ford's Theater, a lock of hair snipped at his deathbed, and, yuckier still, a bloody towel used to daub his gunshot wound. See a statue of the young rail-splitter standing on a flatboat with a pig and a chicken. Tap your toe while a player piano plinks out *Skip to My Lou*, Lincoln's favorite ditty. Watch a special edition of *At the Movies* where Gene Siskel reviews Hollywood's portrayal of Abe Lincoln.

And would any nonprofit museum ever be complete without asking for donations as you exit? Well, *here* the hat they pass is a genuine stovepipe . . . carefully protected with a clear plastic liner.

200 E. Berry St., PO Box 7838, Fort Wayne, IN 46801-7838

(260) 455-3864

Hours: Tuesday–Saturday, 10 A.M.–5 P.M., Sunday 1–5 P.M.

Cost: Adults $2.99, Seniors $1.99, Kids (5–12) $1.99 (You get a Lincoln penny for change!)

www.TheLincolnMuseum.org

Directions: Downtown on Berry St. at Clinton St. (Rte. 27).

FORT WAYNE

A diamond-shaped UFO was spotted by a man and his son near the Fort Wayne Airport on September 11, 1999. The pair grew very thirsty after the encounter, and one developed a kidney infection a week later.

Actress **Carole Lombard** was born Jane Alice Peters on October 6, 1908, in Fort Wayne. Her birth site still stands at 704 Rockhill Street.

"Machine Gun" Kelly's gang robbed the Broadway State Bank (Broadway & Taylor Sts.) in 1930.

Actor **Dick York,** star of TV's *Bewitched*, was born in Fort Wayne on September 4, 1928.

Fort Wayne was once known as Tightwee Village.

Philo T. Farnsworth TV Museum

Several episodes of the sitcom *Seinfeld* deal with Frank Costanza's manic devotion to his lifetime collection of *TV Guides*. If they seem hard to believe, you might want to stop by the Philo T. Farnsworth TV Museum. Lovingly presented in glass cases lining the walls of this miniature museum is every issue of *TV Guide* ever published, "painstakingly put together by Stephen Hofer, Ph.D., over 11 years." The good doctor's Fall Previews have been turned outward to show their covers, but the remaining copies are displayed like a library.

As if the guides weren't special enough, the room is filled with ancient picture tubes (removed from their chassis) and pop culture artifacts from TV shows long gone: PeeWee action figures, *Little House on the Prairie* and *Waltons* games, *Gong Show* candy, Betty White trading cards, a book titled *Barbecuing Dick Van Dyke Style*, a Mork from Ork Eggship Radio, and thousands of other boob tube treasures.

Karen's Antique Mall, 1510 Fairfield Ave., Fort Wayne, IN 46802

(260) 422-4030

Hours: Monday–Saturday 10 A.M.–6 P.M., Sunday 1–5 P.M.

Cost: Free

Directions: Five blocks west of Clinton St. (Rte. 27), three blocks south of Jefferson Blvd., at the railroad overpass.

Gary
Gary, First in Flight

Wright Brothers . . . bah! If you really want to see where heavier-than-air flight originated, you won't travel to the beaches of Kitty Hawk, but to Gary's Marquette Park on the shore of Lake Michigan. It was here at Miller Beach, on June 22, August 20, and September 11, 1896, that Octave Chanute flew the world's first large biplane gliders. Locals were unimpressed and called him "the crazy man of the dunes."

Chanute was a naturalized American, born in Paris, who retired young from a career as a civil engineer to pursue his goal of solving the riddle of human flight. Chanute was neither shy nor secretive about his findings, and he would eventually advise the Wright Brothers—*seven years later*—in 1903, when they flew their now-famous craft in North Carolina.

Few people except aviation nuts even remember Chanute today, but a stone monument outlining his accomplishments sits in Gary's Marquette Park, the approximate location where his gliders lifted free of the dunes. A full-size model of a Chanute glider hangs in the Lake County Convention and Visitors Bureau in nearby Hammond.

Marquette Park, Grand Blvd. & Forest Ave., Gary, IN 46403

No phone

Hours: Daily 8 A.M.–10 P.M.

Cost: Free

Directions: A boulder marker lies south of the park pavilion, at the lakefront.

Lake County Convention and Visitors Bureau, 1770 Corinne Dr., Hammond, IN 46323

(800) ALL-LAKE

Hours: Monday–Friday 8 A.M. –6 P.M., Saturday–Sunday 9 A.M. –6 P.M.

Cost: Free

www.alllake.org

Directions: Kennedy Ave. Exit south from I-80/94, turn right at the first stoplight.

GARY

Gary is the largest U.S. city founded in the 20th century. It was incorporated on July 14, 1906, by U.S. Steel and named after its Chairman of the Board, Judge Elbert H. Gary.

During World War II, civil defense planners worked out a plan to blanket the city with smoke to obscure the city from enemy attack. Apparently, nobody has ever been told the war is over.

More than 1,000 manhole covers disappeared from the streets of Gary in 1992. Each weighed about 100 pounds.

Actor **Karl Malden** was born Malden Sekulovich in Gary on March 22, 1913. He attended Emerson High School, graduating in 1931.

Beat it!

Jackson 5 Sites

Several years ago there was a push to commemorate Michael Jackson on a license plate available for Hoosier drivers. It was doubtful many plates would have been purchased outside of Gary, the singer's hometown. The legislation needed to issue the plates suffered the same fate as a 1995 plan for a Gary-based Jacksons theme park: nobody bought into the idea.

Clearly, if you want to acknowledge the Jackson 5's contribution to this steel city, you have to do it on your own. The first place to start is the former Jackson family home located, strictly by coincidence, on Jackson Street.

Between 1950 and 1966, Joe and Katherine Jackson had nine children: Reebie, Jackie, Tito, Jermaine, LaToya, Marlon, Michael, Randy, and Janet. By all accounts, life in the Jackson household was no picnic. Joe was the classic stage dad, driving the kids to fulfill his own failed musical ambition. Joe had played guitar for the Falcons, a band composed of workers at the Inland Steel Company, to earn extra money. While Joe was at one of his many jobs, a few of his sons began playing with his guitar. He eventually heard them, realized they had talent, and the rest was history.

The Jacksons were not allowed to hang out with local kids. Joe made them practice, practice, practice—four hours a day in addition to their schoolwork. He paced in front of the band carrying a bull whip and would assault them if they flubbed a routine. Joe loved guns, and even "fired" an empty shot from a .38 revolver at Michael when the kid laughed at his father's dancing. At night he would terrorize the youngsters by popping out of a closet wearing a Halloween mask, or standing at the kids' window holding a butcher knife. Fame doesn't come without a price. . . .

Katherine let Joe run the family six days a week, but on Sunday, she was in charge, marching the kids off to the local Jehovah's Witness Kingdom Hall. Today the Jacksons' former church is the Pentacostal Church of God (3435 W. 21st Ave.).

Jackson Family Home, 2300 Jackson St., Gary, IN 46407
Private phone
Hours: Always visible; view from street
Cost: Free
meetthefamily.online.fr
Directions: Just south of 23rd St., six blocks west of Broadway.

Though he was the youngest member of the group, Michael was a standout. He made his first public performance in 1963 at the age of five, just down the street at Garnett Elementary. He sang "Climb Every Mountain," and those who heard it claimed the crowd went wild. Tears streamed down the adults' faces. A star was born!

Garnett Elementary School (now Adult Education Center), 2131 Jackson St., Gary, IN 46407
Private phone
Hours: Always visible; view from street

Cost: Free

Directions: Two blocks north of the Jackson Home.

Michael had started on the bongos, but his Garnett Elementary performance made Joe bump Jermaine as lead singer. The band was named the Ripples and Waves Plus Michael when they won their first amateur music competition singing "My Girl" and "Barefootin'" at the Theodore Roosevelt High School gym.

Theodore Roosevelt High School, 730 W. 25th Ave., Gary, IN 46407

Private phone

Hours: Always visible; view from street

Cost: Free

Directions: One block west and two blocks south of the Jackson Home.

Renamed the Jackson 5, their first professional gig came at Mr. Lucky's Lounge, a Gary bar. All the band members were underage at the time; Michael was only six. Before long, they were playing at saloons and nightclubs all over the region. One of their signature acts was to have little Michael disappear into the audience and reappear beneath a female patron's dress. Eventually they caught the eye of Berry Gordy, president of Motown Records. After cutting their first album, Joe took the group to California, leaving Katherine behind with the rest of the kids.

Mr. Lucky's Lounge (now Mr. Lucky's Liquor), 1100 Grant St., Gary, IN 46404

(219) 885-9095

Hours: Always visible

Cost: Free

Directions: Six blocks south of Rte. 20, at 11th Ave.

HAMMOND

If you stand still and look lazy in Hammond, you are loitering.

You will receive castor oil as punishment if you spit watermelon seeds on the streets of Hammond.

Geneva, Nappanee, Shipshewana
Amish Mania

Northwestern Indiana has well-established populations of both Amish and Mennonites and, with them, a large selection of sightseeing possibilities. Don't risk sideswiping a buggy by rushing to see them all in one weekend— take a hint from the local folk: if you want to maximize your humble, back-to-the-land weekend, choose the Amish attraction that's right for you.

Amishville, U.S.A.

When it comes to the Amish experience, this place might take the theme too far. Amishville, U.S.A. is a 120-acre working farm, where visitors are allowed to look in on all the cow-milking action. They've got buggy rides in the summer and sleigh rides in the winter. Two nonfarm buildings house a gift shop and a restaurant, Der Essen Platz.

The whole operation takes an hour or so to fully appreciate, which is good if you're in a hurry to move on, but bad if you're trying to make a weekend of it.

Amishville, U.S.A., 844 E. County Road 900S, Geneva, IN 46740

(260) 589-3536

E-mail: information@amishville.com

Hours: Monday–Saturday 9 A.M. –5 P.M., Sunday 1–5 P.M.

Cost: Adults $2.75, Kids $1.50, Buggy rides $1.25

www.amishville.com

Directions: County Road 900S east from Rte. 27, follow the signs.

Amish Acres

Amish Acres is like Vegas for folks in black hats and bonnets. The grounds cover 80 acres, a complete farming community with a bakery, meat and cheese shop, cow shed, barn, and white clapboard home. Check out the candle dipping, quilting, fudge making, and horse shoeing before you settle down at the Restaurant Barn for a traditional 12-course meal.

But that's not all! Amish Acres has Indiana's only resident musical repertory theater. It's longest running production, *Plain and Fancy*, is a toe-tapping salute to life among the Amish. Had enough of the beards and button-free outfits? How about *Carnival!*, or racier still, *Gypsy*, or *Damn Yankees*?

Go ahead—spend the night! This place has two hotels, the Nappanee Inn and the Inn at Amish Acres. Both offer large swimming pools, full-body massages, and electricity. They even have a helicopter landing field! Who ever thought living simple could be so scrumptious!??!?

Amish Acres, 1600 W. Market St., Nappanee, IN 46550

(800) 800-4942 or (574) 773-4188

E-mail: AmishAcres@AmishAcres.com

Hours: April–October, Monday–Saturday 7 A.M. –8 P.M., Sunday 10 A.M. –6 P.M.; March, Friday–Saturday 10 A.M. –7 P.M., Sunday 11 A.M. –6 P.M.; November–December, Tuesday–Saturday 10 A.M. –7 P.M., Sunday 10 A.M. –6 P.M.

Cost: Adults $6.95–$8.95, Kids $2.95–$4.95

www.amishacres.com

Directions: One mile west of Rte. 19 on Rte. 6.

Menno-Hof Mennonite-Amish Visitors Center

If Amish Acres is Vegas for buggy drivers, the Menno-Hof Visitors Center is the Smithsonian. Follow the development of the Anabaptist tradition, from 1525 to the present, through its three main branches: the Hutterites, the Mennonites, and the Amish.

While their beliefs stress simplicity, this multimedia extravaganza is anything but! It all starts with the "Good Fences Make Good Community" slide show, then you're whisked back in time to a Zurich courtyard where it all began. The Anabaptists' breakaway from the Roman Catholic Church didn't come without a price, as you'll see in the next room, the Dungeon. Be sure to look down the stone shaft to see the poor soul awaiting his fate for his faith.

Time to get out of town—to the New World! Move through the Harbor to the Sailing Ship, headed for the American colonies. Finish your tour with displays of modern (if that's the word) Anabaptist teachings and activities. No trip through the barn/museum would be complete without a visit to the Tornado Theater. This simulator recalls the Midwest's 1965 Palm Sunday tornado outbreak and Hurricane Joan, which slammed into Nicaragua, with blowing wind, shaking floor, and flashing "lightning."

510 S. Van Buren St., PO Box 701, Shipshewana, IN 46565

(260) 768-4117

E-mail: mennohof@tin.net

Hours: Monday–Saturday 10 A.M. –5 P.M.

Cost: Adults $3, Kids (6–14) $2

www.mennohof.org

Directions: At the south end of town on Rte. 5 (Van Buren St.).

Highland
Devil, Be Gone!

Have you been on the road a while, and the kids seem . . . well . . . *rowdier* than usual? Don't be so quick to blame it on that junk food pit stop in Muncie. Did you ever consider that the little ones might be POSSESSED??!!?

Sure you have. So, why not bring them by the Hegewisch Baptist Church to drive out those demons? That's right: exorcism. Given its recent association with pea soup and spinning heads, they don't call the practice "exorcism," but "Demonic Deliverance."

HBC Pastor Win Worley began the practice in 1970, but not until 1992 did this place hold an open house. They got more than 500 visitors, mostly from this world. Today, they host several Deliverance Meetings a year, and if you promise to sit through an entire Sunday service, they'll cleanse your soul on the way out. To find out about their next Deliverance Meeting, check out their Web site. There you'll find do-it-yourself Deliverance prayers (just fill in the possessed's name in the blanks), HBC's perspectives on rock music (including ABBA), their Plan of Salvation, and FAQs.

Hegewisch Baptist Church of Highland, 8711 Cottage Grove Rd., PO Box 9327, Highland, IN 46322

(219) 838-9410

E-mail: info@hbcdelivers.org

Hours: Thursday 7 P.M., Sunday 10:30 A.M. and 6 P.M.

Cost: Regular services, free; four-day workshops $17

www.hbcdelivers.org

Directions: One block north of Rte. 6, 11 blocks east of Rte. 41.

ISLAND PARK
A monster with a two-foot-wide head was spotted in Big Chapman Lake at Island Park in 1934. It had "cow-like" eyes.

Huntington
The Dan Quayle Center and Museum

The residents of Huntington felt a museum was the least they could do for their most famous native son, so they converted an old Christian Science Church and stuffed it with Quayle-abilia. Upstairs, you can see the Quayle clan's family heirlooms: a lock of Danny's baby hair, his Little League uniform, and his Senate golf bag, well used. And be sure to check out the report cards from his stellar elementary school career. Every visitor wants to see what grades he received in Spelling!

The museum also has Quayle's Indiana University law degree, chewed by Barnaby, the family dog. Barnaby was put up for adoption shortly after the incident. True story—Marilyn doesn't mess around. One of the strangest artifacts is a hollow ostrich egg with Quayle's veep inauguration re-created inside, faithfully depicting Marilyn's infamous blue UFO hat. It was made by a Quayle supporter. And be sure to get your photo taken next to a life-size cutout of the Boy Wonder; let your pose reflect your political persuasion.

The ground floor of the museum is filled with items relating to all of the nation's Second Bananas. More veeps have come from Indiana than any other state, earning it the nickname "Birthplace of Vice Presidents": Schuyler Colfax, Thomas Hendricks, Charles Warren Fairbanks, Thomas Marshall (who said, "What this country needs is a really good five-cent cigar"), and Dan Quayle.

815 Warren St., PO Box 856, Huntington, IN 46750

(260) 356-6356

E-mail: info@quaylemuseum.org

Hours: Tuesday–Saturday 10 A.M. –4 P.M., Sunday 1–4 P.M.

Cost: Adults $3, Kids $1.50, Families $9

www.quaylemuseum.org

Directions: At Warren & Tipton (Rte. 24) Sts., one block east of Rte. 224.

The Real Quayle Trail

Would you like to go "hunting" Quayle? Strange as it sounds, the museum dedicated to this right-wing bird will give you directions, though the trail is kind of cold. A Quayle Trail tour is offered to tour buses and large groups interested in the former veep; and since there are so few tourists that qualify, this guidebook offers a few local highlights from Dan's life, not all of which you'll find on the sanctioned tour.

First off, as you drive into Huntington, ask yourself why this middling town has a four-lane beltway, a superhighway connecting it to Fort Wayne, and so many beautiful, government-funded projects? When Dan Quayle rails at "tax-and-spend Democrats," remember his home town, a pork-barrel burg if ever there was one.

Stop 1: Dan Quayle's Boyhood Home

It's there . . . if you're interested. Though born in Indianapolis on February 4, 1947, Dan and his family lived in this humble home from 1950 to 1955. His bedroom was located in the back left corner. Dan was four when they moved to town, nine when they packed up for Arizona and that infamous home on the golf course.

On the morning of the kickoff rally for the Bush–Quayle ticket in 1988, Dan and Marilyn dropped by to look at his old home before heading over to the county courthouse.

1317 Polk, Huntington, IN 46750

Private phone

Hours: Always visible; view from street

Cost: Free

Directions: Head southeast on Rte. 224 from Rte. 24, turn right on McGahn St., five blocks to
  Polk St. and turn left.

Stop 2: Dan Quayle's High School

The Quayle family returned to Huntington in 1963 where Dan attended, and eventually graduated from, Huntington High School. He was president of the Teen-Age Republicans. Not surprisingly, he was also on the golf team. Dan graduated in 1965 and went off to DePauw in Greencastle.

Crestview Middle School (former Huntington High School), 929 Guilford, Huntington, IN 46750

(260) 356-6210

Hours: Always visible

Cost: Free

Directions: Two blocks east of Jefferson St. (Rte. 224) at Tipton St.

Stop 3: Dan Quayle's Hometown National Guard

On turning 18, young Dan was eligible to be drafted. Like most young men of the time, he could be shipped off to Vietnam . . . unless that certain young man had (1) a student deferment, and (2) family connections to get him into the National Guard after that deferment ran out. Dan had both.

After graduating from DePauw and facing the end of his deferment, Quayle called his father. Dad had connections to Wendell Phillippi, retired major general of the Indiana National Guard, who felt that young Dan was just the Guard's type of recruit: the son of one of his politically connected friends. Quayle served as typist for the quarterly *Indiana National Guardsman* as part of the 120th Public Information Detachment. (Dan's Guard service was the basis of a recurring jokes of his political career: What do you get when you cross a hawk with a chicken? A Quayle!)

Fellow Guardsman James Newland, Jr. explained the Public Information Detachment's service this way: "We had some free time and it wasn't odd for us to drink some beer and play cards during an extended lunch break or after drill. . . . we never failed to have a good time." When Quayle was released from service he took a test on "Fundamentals of Writing" and "Army Information." He scored a 56.

National Guard Armory, 800 Zahn St., Huntington, IN 46750

(260) 356-5806

Hours: Always visible

Cost: Free

Directions: Seven blocks west of Rte. 224, four blocks north of Rte. 24 Business.

Stop 4: Dan and Marilyn Come to Town

Quayle returned to Huntington for a third time following law school, this time with his new wife, Marilyn. They opened a law practice in 1974, though Marilyn did most of the legal work. Dan was an associate publisher on the family-owned local paper. When asked if she was smarter than her hubby, Marilyn said, "I would not have married Dan Quayle had I not thought he was an equal to me."

In 1976, Quayle was asked by the Republican county chairman to run for congress, and told the official, "I'll have to check with my dad." His father threw Dan all the support he could muster when his son broke the news. "Go ahead, you won't win," he said.

Quayle won anyway. Marilyn later reflected on the campaign, "I made all the decisions." He served two terms in the House, where fellow congressmen called him "Wet Head" because he always seemed to be coming from the gym.

He was then elected to the Senate in 1980, beating incumbent Birch Bayh, who had to eat his own words: "C'mon boys, don't bother me. I'm debating Dan Quayle. The boy's retarded." Dan said there were some disadvantages to the office: "[In the House] you can get a bunch of guys and go down to the gym and play basketball. You can't do that in the Senate."

When Dan wasn't in Washington at the Senate gym, he was back in Huntington. He developed a taste for breaded tenderloin sandwiches at Nick's Kitchen, officially known as "Dan Quayle's Favorite Restaurant." OK, so it's not like getting endorsed by Julia Child, but around here (if nowhere else), Dan's opinion means something. Nick's has returned the favor, and now has a Quayleburger on the menu.

Nick's Kitchen, 506 N. Jefferson St., Huntington, IN 46750

(260) 356-6618

Hours: Monday–Friday 5:30 A.M. –2 P.M., 4–8 P.M., Saturday 5:30 A.M. –2 P.M.

Cost: Meals $4–$8

Directions: On Rte. 24, downtown.

Stop 5: Dan Quayle, VP Candidate

It was one of the most candid things Quayle ever said. Shortly after being tapped by George Bush as the vice-presidential candidate, word got out of his unique treatment during the Vietnam War. "I didn't know in 1969 that I would be in this room today, I'll confess," he told the bloodthirsty reporters.

The first rally with both Bush and Quayle took place on the steps of the Huntington County Courthouse. While George Bush once claimed, "We cannot gamble with inexperience in that Oval Office," there was no longer any talk like that. Ix-nay on the ambling-gay! George Bush later summed up his professional empathy for his running mate: "Take out the word Quayle and insert the word Bush wherever it appears, and that's the crap I took for eight years. Wimp. Sycophant. Lap dog. Poop. Lightweight. Boob. Squirrel. Asshole. George Bush." Good point.

Huntington County Courthouse, 201 N. Jefferson St., Huntington, IN 46750

(260) 358-4814

Hours: Always visible

Cost: Free

Directions: On Jefferson St. (Rte. 224), downtown.

QUAYLE-ISMS

Dan Quayle is to politics what Yogi Berra was to baseball—an eloquent spokesperson. Here are a few of his most famous thoughts."

➡ "People that are really very weird can get into sensitive positions and have tremendous impact on history."

➡ "I deserve respect for the things I did not do."

➡ "Verbosity leads to unclear, inarticulate things."

➡ "We're going to have the best-educated American people in the world."

➡ "[Republicans] understand the importance of bondage between parent and child."

➡ "One word sums up probably the responsibility of any vice president, and that one word is 'to be prepared.'"

➡ "Hawaii has always been a very pivotal role in the Pacific. It is in the Pacific. It is part of the United States that is an island that is right here."

➡ "If we don't succeed, we run the risk of failure."

➡ "I used to be a Batman fan until I had this job [VP]; now all of a sudden Robin looks awfully good."

➡ (On the environment) "It isn't pollution that's harming our environment. It's the impurities in the air and water that are doing it."

➡ (On the United Negro College Fund) "What a waste it is to lose one's mind—or not to have a mind is being truly wasteful. How true that is."

➡ (On education) "Quite frankly, teachers are the only profession that teach our children."

➡ (On space) "Mars is in essentially the same orbit. Mars is somewhat the same distance from the sun, which is very important. We have seen pictures where there are canals, we believe, and water. If there is water, that means there is oxygen. If oxygen, that means we can breathe."

➡ (On the Indy 500 while asking the Secretary of Transportation to invite him to the event) "Vrooom! Vrroooom! Vrrroooooom!"

➡ "I stand by all the misstatements that I've made."

Kendallville
Mid-America Windmill Museum

In the history of the settlement of the Great Plains, the windmill's contribution often gets short shrift. Not in Kendallville. This specialty museum honors the wind-powered workhorses that pumped the water and milled the grain that made American agriculture possible.

The windmill collection was started by Russ Baker and now contains more than 30 restored windmills along a strolling pathway. Kendallville was chosen for the location of this museum because the area was once home to many windmill manufacturers. If you visit in late June, you may even see a windmill erected and blown for the annual Windmill Festival. Have no fear—it's not as dirty as it sounds.

Allen Chapel Rd. & Wallace Dr., PO Box 5048, Kendallville, IN 46755

(260) 347-2334

E-mail: corbake@ligtel.com

Hours: May–October, Tuesday–Friday 10 A.M. –4 P.M., Saturday 10 A.M. –5 P.M., Sunday 1–4 P.M.

Cost: Adults $3, Seniors $2.50, Kids (6–12) $1.50

www.noblecan.org/~kpc/wind/

Directions: West of town on Rte. 6, turn south on County Rd. 1000E, follow the signs.

Big, bad Belle. Photo by Patrick Hughes, courtesy of the La Porte County Historical Society Museum

La Porte
Belle Was a Groundbreaker

In many ways, Belle Gunness broke new ground for American women. Long before women achieved universal suffrage, Gunness proved that a determined woman could do anything a man could, at least in her chosen profession: serial murderer. Born in Norway in 1858, she emigrated to the States in 1886 and settled near Chicago. She married Mads Sorenson in 1893 and adopted several children who, shortly after Belle received money for their care, mysteriously died. Then Mads perished in a fit of convulsions in 1900. Belle bought a pig farm outside La Porte with her husband's life insurance settlement.

She didn't stay single long. Belle married Peter Gunness in 1902, but he died eight months later when a coffee grinder fell from a high shelf and crushed his skull. Again, Belle received a healthy insurance settlement. Hmmmm. . . .

Worried she might begin to develop a reputation among suspicious insurance agents, Belle devised a new fundraising plan. She advertised in Chicago's Norwegian "lonely hearts" newspapers for a spouse, and managed to convince her suitors to liquidate their assets and head to La Porte, cash in hand. "And don't tell your family where you're headed," she'd add in her perfumed letters, "it would ruin the surprise when we tie the knot!"

Disposing of the bodies became an awful chore, so she had a hired hand, Ray Lamphere, dig ditches for her to bury her "trash." Many mornings Lampere would find the ditches filled back in. He was starting to become suspicious at the late-night departures (reported by Belle, but never witnessed by him) of so many of Belle's potential husbands. Why did they always leave their belongings?

The brother of one suitor, A. K. Helgelein, came looking for his sibling, having written Belle in advance. The day before he arrived, Belle made up a will with a local attorney. That night, April 28, 1908, her home burned to the ground, killing Belle and three children she had produced or collected along the way.

Ray Lamphere was charged with arson and murder, but after 13 bodies were unearthed, Belle looked more like a suspect than a victim. Still, Lamphere was convicted of arson and spent the rest of his life in the Michigan City penitentiary.

Was Belle the headless body found in the burned home? Officials claimed it was considerably smaller than the robust Belle, and its only identifying feature was a charred dental plate found in the rubble. Many historians today believe Gunness escaped by killing a prostitute, beheading her, and leaving her own dentures with the body before lighting a cover-up fire.

The excavation of the victims of "Lady Bluebeard" became a popular pastime in pre-television, pre-radio La Porte. Families would come out to watch the diggings and carve their initials on an unburned shed on the property. You can view the graffiti-marked shed today in the La Porte County Historical Society Museum. Inside is a scary, crude mannequin of Belle. You'll see sketches of the farm, the letter and four-leaf clover Gunness sent to Helgelein, and a gruesome photo of victim Ole Budsberg's head as it was brought in to Lamphere's trial on a shovel—also available as a postcard at the front desk. A plaque in the shed repeats a popular rhyme of the time:

> Amid roses of red
> & violets of blue,
> She buried not one,
> But forty-two.

Forty-two? Fourteen? Exactly how victims many did she off? It's hard to tell, but somewhere between 14 and 40 men bought the farm on the farm

Belle bought. A. K. Helgelein was buried in Patton Cemetery in La Porte (McCollum & Rumely Sts.), and his tombstone indicates his status as Gunness's final victim.

Gunness Farm, McClung Rd., La Porte, IN 46350

No phone

Hours: Always visible; view from the road

Cost: Free

Directions: North from downtown on Rte. 35/39 until the routes diverge, follow Rte. 39 and take the first right onto McClung Rd., follow McClung north along Fishtrap Lake until you see a gate with "No Dumping" signs on the left; her home was where the field to the west is today.

La Porte County Historical Society Museum, 809 State St., La Porte, IN 46350

(219) 326-6808 x276

Hours: Tuesday–Saturday 10 A.M.–4:30 P.M.

Cost: Free

www.lapcohistsoc.org/belleg1.htm

Directions: Next to the courthouse on the north side of Independence Plaza.

Ligonier
Indiana Historical Radio Museum

Housed in a former filling station, the Indiana Historical Radio Museum is a small but impressive collection of wireless technology from an era before cell phones. More than 400 antique radios are on display, from gigantic wooden cabinets made in the 1920s to the first transistor radios, including novelty items like Budweiser beer can radios and funky, plastic disco-era receivers.

Not all the radios conjure innocent memories of Charlie McCarthy and Edgar Bergen; check out the model from Nazi Germany, used no doubt to listen to evil diatribes on world domination. And be sure to try your hand at tuning an old-style set. It took three finely tuned knobs to receive a transmission. Try to do *that* while driving your car.

800 Lincolnway South, Ligonier, IN 46767-0353

(888) 417-3562 or (260) 894-9000

E-mail: olradio@ligtel.com

Hours: May–October, Tuesday–Wednesday, Friday–Saturday 10 A.M. –2 P.M.; November–April, Saturday 10 A.M. –2 P.M.

Cost: Free

home.att.net/~indianahistoricalradio/ihrp6mus.htm

Directions: Where Rte. 5 (Lincolnway South) meets Union St., north of downtown.

Logansport
Catch the Brass Ring

Were it not for lawyers, there might be more brass ring carousels in the United States today. All those riders risking their necks, leaning out to grab a brass ring for a free ride, turned ambulance chasers into merry-go-round monitors. But the good folk of Logansport are sticking to their rings.

The Cass County Carousel was built in 1902 (some say 1885) by Gustav Dentzel in Fort Wayne, then moved to Logansport in 1919. It was restored in 1993, and is the only surviving brass ring merry-go-round in the state. Most of its 42 hand-carved critters are horses, but they've also got deer, giraffes, goats, a lion, and a tiger. The two felines don't move up and down, making it much easier to reach for the round golden object of your desire.

Lest you think this throwback is unaffected by the litigious who walk among us, check out the animals on the outside track. They all have seat belts.

Cass County Carousel, McHale Community Complex, Riverside Park, 1208 Riverside Dr., Logansport, IN 46947

(574) 753-8725

Hours: June–August, Monday–Friday 6–9 P.M., Saturday–Sunday 1–9 P.M.; September–October, Saturday–Sunday 1–5 P.M.

Cost: 50¢/ride, or one brass ring

www.cassarts.org/cass_county_dentzel_carousel.htm

Directions: Five blocks east of Rte. 25, four blocks north of Rte. 24, between 10th and 11th Sts.

LOGANSPORT

Actor **Greg Kinnear** was born in Logansport on June 17, 1963.

LOWELL

Comedienne **Jo Anne Worley** of *Laugh-In* fame was born in Lowell on September 6, 1937.

This must have hurt.

Mentone
World's Largest Egg

As hard-boiled eggs go, this is one of the hardest—concrete, no less. Built in 1946 by Hugh Rickel and weighing a ton and a half, the 11-foot Mentone Egg honors the region's primary agricultural export. Mentone calls itself the "Egg Basket of the Midwest," and if all the hens laid them this large, they'd need some mighty big baskets. Every June, the town throws an Egg Festival, and it recently tried to raise enough funds to construct an egg-shaped water tower. They were unsuccessful, so this oversized ova will have to do for now.

The question that comes to mind while admiring this 3,000-pound monument is one that has puzzled philosophers for centuries: Which came first, the concrete chicken or the concrete egg? Well, nobody around here has ever seen a cement chicken!

E. Main & Morgan Sts., PO Box 365, Mentone, IN 46539

(800) 800-6090 or (260) 353-7417

Hours: Always visible

Cost: Free

Directions: Near the grain elevator at the corner of Main (Rte. 25) and Morgan Sts.

MICHIGAN CITY
A 26-year-old man, standing atop Mt. Baldy, spotted a UFO on the sands of Indiana Dunes State Park on December 21, 2000. He also claimed that he had "lost" two hours of memory that evening.

Over $300,000 worth of whiskey is believed to have been buried by **Al Capone**'s gang in a cave on Lake Michigan near Michigan City. The entrance was closed with dynamite and has never been discovered.

A "wild child" haunts Fish Lake in Michigan City. It was first spotted in 1839, and has been howling ever since.

Actress **Anne Baxter** was born in Michigan City on May 7, 1923.

MISHAWAKA
Mishawaka is Potawatomi for "dead trees place," so named because founders cleared a forest to erect the town.

PLYMOUTH
The water from a well near Plymouth reportedly once had magnetic qualities; any steel object placed in the water would turn magnetic. It has since gone dry.

Michigan City
Submarine Superstar

If you were asked, "Where would be a good location for a submarine base?" would you answer, "Indiana"? You would if you were Lodner Phillips! When this former cobbler began asking the same question of the U.S. Navy, the answer was more likely, "What's a submarine?" Large underwater craft had yet to be invented, and the Navy was not convinced that a submarine was even militarily useful.

Phillips set out to change the Navy's mind. Between 1840 and 1850 he built several vessels. The first was a small one-man craft, but later models were 40 feet long. The full-sized subs could dive 100 feet below the surface of Lake Michigan, which is exactly what he did with his family on weekends.

Phillips was awarded more than 40 patents for his maritime inventions, which included torpedoes, underwater suits, and diving bells. But, due in part to the distraction of the Civil War, he never persuaded the Navy to build a port in Indiana. He eventually left town for New York, and would be forgotten in Michigan City today were it not for several models of his Hoosier inventions on display at its Lighthouse Museum. The museum also has a large collection of ship models, old postcards, and lighthouse gewgaws.

Old Lighthouse Museum, Washington Park, Heisman Harbor Rd., PO Box 512,
   Michigan City, IN 46360

(219) 872-6133

Hours: Tuesday–Sunday 1–4 P.M.

Cost: Adults $2, Kids (5–12) 50¢

Directions: Just west of Franklin St. (the continuation of Pine St.), at the lake.

PORTAGE
Each October, Portage hosts Elvis FANtasy Fest for the King's fans.
Call (800) 283-8687.

Looking for Mary in an aboveground cave.
Photo by Patrick Hughes, courtesy of the Carmelite Shrines

Munster
Carmelite Shrines

Northern Indiana is, in a word, FLAT. This geographic reality makes it all the more difficult to find a cave in which to establish a grotto. But the parishioners at the Carmelite Shrines in Munster didn't let the topography get them *down,* they just built their caves *up.*

The exterior of the Main Grotto hardly does justice to the treasures that lie within. Just to the right of the main, exterior altar is a small, candle-filled niche that opens to yet another, larger room, and another, and another, and another. The walls are covered in rough stones embedded in concrete, and broken by marble bas-reliefs of biblical scenes. Your holy journey is illuminated by recessed lighting and backlit onyx sconces. Find the stairs to the second floor and you can peep out a secret window aimed at a statue of the Virgin. The final grotto has dozens of scenes carved to show Mary in all her incarnations: Mother Undefiled, Mother Most Amiable, Mother Most Admirable, Mother of This, Mother of That . . .

At the north end of the gardens, another grotto is sunken into the ground like a crypt. It functions as a chapel, and the clammy subterranean aura seems all the more spooky when you come across a death-sized statue of Jesus, sprawled out on the altar. Yikes!

1628 Ridge Rd., Munster, IN 46321

(219) 838-7111

Hours: Daily 9 A.M.–6 P.M.; call ahead to have the lights turned on.

Cost: Free

Directions: Eight blocks west of Rte. 41, on the south side of the road.

If you had an airplane, why would you drive a Studebaker?
Courtesy of Bendix Woods County Park

New Carlisle
World's Largest Living Sign

Strange as it sounds, the World's Largest Living Sign promotes a product that is not currently available to a consumer base that, on the whole, can't appreciate it. In 1938, gardeners planted 8,259 white pines on the Studebaker automobile proving grounds west of South Bend. The trees were arranged to form letters spelling out "STUDEBAKER" when viewed from the air. Each letter is 200 feet wide and 200 feet long. The trees have grown 60 feet tall. To fully appreciate the living sign you must fly over the old racetrack, now part of a park currently known as Bendix Woods, and pick out the brand name in the sculpted treetops.

Bendix Woods County Park, 32132 State Road 2, New Carlisle, IN 46552

(574) 654-3155

Hours: Monday–Friday 8 A.M.–4:30 P.M., Saturday 1–4:30 P.M.

Cost: In-state, $2/car; Out-of-state, $3/car

www.sjcparks.org/bendix.html

Directions: On the south side of Western Ave. (Rte. 2), just east of the county line.

Peru
Circus Museum

Most parents would cringe at the thought of their child running away to join the circus, but not in Peru. Kids here are actually *encouraged* to become circus performers, and they don't even have to run away— Peru already is "The Circus City."

Peru's circus tradition began in 1884 when Ben Wallace and James Anderson purchased the W. C. Coup Circus at auction and renamed it "Wallace & Co.'s Great World Menagerie, Grand International Mardi Gras, Highway Holiday Hidalgo, and Alliance of Novelties." Who *wouldn't* buy tickets for that? Season after season, Wallace bought out or merged with other shows, and the whole operation wintered at an elaborate facility on the east bank of the Mississinewa River, 2.5 miles east of town. (Drive east on Rte. 124, and turn left just after crossing the bridge to see crumbling remnants of the headquarters.)

In 1907, Wallace bought the Carl Hagenbeck Circus, forming the Hagenbeck-Wallace Circus, the best-known touring operation stationed in Peru. Over the next 30 years (under a variety of owners) it would employ the likes of Emmett Kelly, Tom Mix, lion tamer Clyde Beatty, the Great Willi Wilno (better known as The Human Cannonball), and Blacaman the Hindoo Animal Hypnotist.

A small museum located downtown in a former circus building is filled with uniforms, posters, harnesses, cages, trapezes, and lots of photos, not to mention Rattlesnake Annie's maracas. On the third weekend in July each year, local residents put on the Circus City Festival. All of the performers are Miami County residents, many of whom are descendants of former performers . . . parents who *wish* their kids would run away with the circus.

Circus City Center, 154 N. Broadway, Peru, IN 46970

(765) 472-7553

Hours: April–September, Monday–Friday 9 A.M.–5 P.M.; October–March, Monday–
Friday 9 A.M.–4 P.M.

Cost: Adults $6, Seniors $5, Kids $4

www.circushalloffame.com

Directions: Downtown at the intersection of 7th St. and Broadway.

Circus City Festival, PO Box 700, Peru, IN 46970

(765) 472-3918

www.perucircus.com

Cole Porter's Birthplace and Grave

Cole Porter was born in Peru on June 9, 1891, and was by all accounts a precocious child. The grandson of one of the richest men in town, J. O. Cole, young master Cole was pampered and indulged from the time he could walk. He returned the attention by composing songs for his mother and staging elaborate performances in the sun porch. When his mother consulted a gypsy about her son's future, she was told that people whose initials spelled out words were prone to greatness; Mom immediately gave her son a middle name: Albert. C. A. P. spells "cap"!

Porter loved growing up in a town of circus performers, and he would often take the Fat Lady for rides around town in his donkey cart, or seek out the Wild Man of Borneo to get the inside scoop on upcoming big-top events. His musical abilities improved as he grew older, and during the summers he would play the piano for passengers aboard the *Peerless*, an excursion boat that sailed the waters of Lake Maxinkuckee. At the age of 14, Porter was sent off to Worcester Academy, a boarding school in Massachusetts.

The composer and lyricist didn't spend much more time in Peru until he returned in an urn 60 years later. He died in California on October 15, 1964, after complications from a kidney stone operation. Porter's birth home still stands, though it is somewhat less glamorous than when the young prodigy lived there. Today, Big Wheels and other toys litter the lawn. Peru celebrates Cole Porter Days each June.

Porter's Birthplace, 102 E. 3rd St., Peru, IN 46970

Private phone

Hours: Always visible

Cost: Free

Directions: Two blocks east of Broadway (Rte. 19) at Huntington St.

Porter's Grave, Mount Hope Cemetery, 411 N. Grant St., Peru, IN 46970

(765) 472-2493

Hours: Daily 8 A.M.–5 P.M.

Cost: Free

Directions: At the corner of N. Grant & W. 12th Sts.

Cole Porter Walking/Driving Tour

Contact: Miami County Museum, 51 N. Broadway, Peru, IN 46970

(765) 473-9183

www.miamicountyin.com/history/cole

Freaks of Nature, and Cole Porter's Hand-Me-Downs

One good thing about living in a town filled with circus-loving folk is that they're not afraid of freaks of nature. Take the stuffed, two-headed calf on the second floor of the Miami County Museum. Born on a local farm, it lived for a few weeks. It's mild in comparison to the one-headed, two-bodied "Siamese" pig standing next to it—and neither holds a candle to the gruesome white dress hanging nearby. It was worn by a local girl when she fell from, and was run over by, her family's wagon. The parents kept the dead child's bloody dress for years before donating it to the museum for all to see.

The ground floor exhibits have their own wonderful weirdness, including the remains of two circus animals. A crudely removed lion pelt, from its nose to the tip of its tail, is draped over a padded stand. In another case are the remains of Charley, a rogue elephant from the Hagenbeck-Wallace Circus. As the museum's brochure says, "Our school children like to hear the story about Big Charley." To make a long story short, in April 1901 this perky pachyderm drowned his cruel trainer, Henry Hoffman, in the Wabash River and had to be destroyed. The museum has Charley's tusk and bullet-riddled skull. Cute story.

Finally, among the dead animals and arrowheads, you can find "artifacts" from Peru's favorite son, Cole Porter—including his 1955 Cadillac, the carrying case for his dog, Hildegarde, and his oversized white sofa.

Miami County Museum, 51 N. Broadway, Peru, IN 46970

(765) 473-9183

E-mail: mchs@netusa1.net

Hours: Tuesday–Saturday 9 A.M.–5 P.M.

Cost: Free

www.netusa1.net/~mchs

Directions: At the corner of Broadway and 6th St.

Rochester
Hoosier Tarzan

When you think of Hollywood's first Tarzan, who comes to mind? Johnny Weissmuller? Try Elmo Linkenhelt! Never heard of him? Perhaps you know him better by his stage name: Elmo Lincoln. Still not ringing a bell? Then come on by the Fulton County Historical Society for an ape-man education.

Lincoln was a Rochester native who moved to California in his teens and was later discovered by director D. W. Griffith. He played bit parts in *The Birth of a Nation* and other less memorable films before being cast as Tarzan in 1918. During filming, Elmo was required to kill a lion named "Old Charlie." The process was made all the easier because the aged cat was heavily drugged. Anything to impress Jane.

Tarzan of the Apes, which made more than $1 million, was followed by *The Romance of Tarzan*. It was a flop. Lincoln went on to different roles, and other actors were tapped to play the Lord of the Apes. But don't forget what type of man it took to fend off that first ferocious feline: a Hoosier.

You can see plenty of Lincoln artifacts at the Fulton County Historical Society, as well as thousands of other curiosities from the region. Everywhere you turn there seem to be creepy, midsize dolls carved by Ray Fretlinger. The museum buildings seem to run on forever, and you begin to wonder if the curators ever throw anything away. The answer is simple. They don't.

Fulton County Historical Society, Round Barn Museum, 37 E. County Road 375N, Rochester, IN 46975

(574) 223-4436
Hours: Monday–Saturday 9 A.M.–5 P.M.
Cost: $1.50 donation
www.icss.net/~fchs
Directions: Four miles north of town on Rte. 31.

Roselawn
Hanging Out in Roselawn

Do you long for those childhood days when you were allowed to run naked and nobody batted an eye? Well, perhaps you ought to come to Roselawn, where not one but *two* nudist resorts are open to the general public: Sun Aura and the Ponderosa Sun Club.

Sun Aura, while under new management, has existed at this location for decades. The camp started as Naked City and was host to the annual Miss Nude America and Miss Nude Teenybopper contests. Back in 1969, they launched the nation's first nude ski area, the "See and Ski" resort. For obvious reasons, it didn't last. Today Sun Aura bills itself as a "family-oriented" nudist colony looking not unlike a KOA Campground, but the old folks in the golf carts aren't wearing any clothes. There's a small lake, a large swimming pool, sand dunes, volleyball courts, and other fun-in-the-sun common areas, as well as an 8,000-square-foot round clubhouse that doesn't look like it has been remodeled since the 1970s. Open year-round, Sun Aura schedules an event every weekend from April through September, including the Mother's Day Dance, Yard Sale Weekend, Pig Roast, and the late season Oldies Dance. Mark those calendars!

Sun Aura does not require that guests be nude, but strongly encourages it. The Ponderosa Sun Club, on the other hand, will only allow you to wear a T-shirt if you've got a really bad sunburn . . . but not pants! No sunburn? No clothes! The Ponderosa Sun Club has a large pool with a split-level sun deck, tennis, volleyball, horseshoe courts, and a central campfire—but be extra careful of flying embers.

Sun Aura, 3449 E. State Rd. 10, Lake Village, IN 46349
(219) 345-2000
Hours: Office 9 A.M.–8 P.M. daily
Cost: Monday–Thursday $20/day; Friday–Sunday $25/day; campsites extra
Directions: West of the railroad tracks on the south side of Rte. 10.

Ponderosa Sun Club, PO Box 305, Roselawn, IN 46372

(219) 345-2268

E-mail: unclub@netnitco.net

Hours: May 15–September 15, Monday–Thursday 9 A.M.–6 P.M., Friday–Saturday
  8 A.M.–8 P.M., Sunday 8 A.M.–6 P.M.

Cost: $25/day; campsites extra

pondersosasunclub.com

Directions: Turn north off Rte. 10, just west of the railroad tracks, and follow the signs
  on County Road 400E.

South Bend
Studebaker National Museum & Archives

Most automotive manufacturers got involved in the transportation indus-
try *after* the invention of the internal combustion engine. Not the Stude-
bakers. These five brothers began making vehicles in 1852, and what a
time to get started! The Civil War was looming, and the nation needed
wagons. Shortly after the smoke had settled, the brothers established the
Studebaker Brothers Manufacturing Company in 1868. Over the next
hundred years, they rolled with the changing market, moving from
prairie schooner wagons to buggies, to autos, to oblivion.

Trace the company's century-long story at this unique museum. You
can also see four different carriages used by U.S. presidents, including the
doom buggy Abraham Lincoln rode to Ford's Theater. Some of the more
popular vehicles here were never available to the public at large, like the
1956 Packard Predictor (a Jetsonesque dreammobile with "Push-Button
Control of Its Ultramatic Transmission"), a push-me, pull-you vehicle
named "Peggy," which shuttled senators between their offices and the U.S.
Capitol; a small prototype of a two-person hovercraft, the Curtis-Wright
Bee; and the last Studebaker to roll off the assembly line on March 17,
1966, a turquoise Timberline. So sad.

Studebaker National Museum, 525 S. Main St., South Bend, IN 46601

(574) 235-9714 or (574) 235-9479

Hours: Monday–Saturday 9 A.M.–5 P.M., Sunday noon–5 P.M.

Cost: Adults $6.50, Seniors $5.50, Kids (3–12) $3.50

www.studebakermuseum.org

Directions: On southbound Rte. 31 (Main St.), 4 blocks south of downtown.

Where the Gipper Croaked

Unlike the fantasy George Gipp portrayed by Ronald Reagan in *Knute Rockne, All-American* in 1940, the real George Gipp was something less than a saint . . . a lot less. He is widely believed to have bet on football games, played poker till all hours of the night, and drunk like a fish. It was one of those bawdy, boozy binges that was his undoing.

Coming home late from a night of gambling, stinking drunk, the Gipper decided to curl up on the back steps of Washington Hall to get a little shut-eye. Or perhaps he passed out—or maybe he was stuck outside after curfew—nobody seems to know for sure. Unfortunately, it was snowing that evening and George caught pneumonia. His lung infection worsened over the next few days, and he died at St. Joseph's Hospital (801 E. LaSalle Ave.) on December 14, 1920. The movie version showed none of that.

A Gipper story almost as believable as the film surrounds his ghost. Though he didn't die there, George's spirit is said to haunt the attic of Washington Hall and has been seen by drama students since the 1970s. Though it is a theater/auditorium today, it was once used as a temporary residence for students that included—you guessed it—George Gipp. He lived on the upper floor, near the attic, and has been making strange noises ever since.

Washington Hall, University of Notre Dame, Notre Dame, IN 46556

(574) 631-8128

Hours: Always visible

Cost: Free

admissions.nd.edu/virtualtour/standard/tour3c.html

Directions: Directly east of the Golden Dome; Gipp slept on the tall staircase in the back, on the north side of the building.

SOUTH BEND
A mysterious shower of fish fell on the northwest side of South Bend in July 1937.

Valparaiso
A New Way of Spelling

Universalist minister William G. Talcott wanted to reform the English language to make spelling simpler—and who can blame him? Think of all the time you'd save if a phone was a fon, and a new gnu was a nu nu! Talcott called his simplified system *phonotypy*, which he perfected during the 1840s. He started off on the right track, dropping such useless letters as K, Q, and X, but before he was done he'd added 16 other characters, each with a unique sound.

As you probably realize, unless you're a very poor speller, phonotypy never caught on. In fact, the only place you can still see it used today is on Talcott's century-old tombstone:

> In memori uv Wm. C. Tolkut ho woz born Des. 25, 1815,
> and died Des. 30, 1902. He hopt kooperativ industri wud prov
> a remedi for poverti. He woz a spelin reformr since 1843
> and prepared dis epitaf in sienst spelin in his lif.

Thank goodness he didn't use any of those strange characters!

Union Cemetery, College Ave. & Union St., Valparaiso, IN 46383

No phone

Hours: Daily 9 A.M.–5 P.M.

Cost: Free

Directions: Four blocks east of Rte. 2, four blocks south of Rte. 130, on the western edge of the cemetery.

Wakarusa
Bird's-Eye View Museum

If you grew up in Wakarusa or Bonneville Grist Mills, DeVon Rose's matchstick creations will remind of the good ol' days. If you've never been to either of these towns, you can experience them through his miniature dioramas. Look! There's the Wayne Feed Mill, and the Eby Ford dealership! And the Bag Factory! Oh, what a fascinating place Wakarusa can be, even when shrunk down to a 1/60 scale.

DeVon Rose started building the Bird's-Eye View Museum as a weekend project in 1967, and he's still at it more than 30 years later. Though you might expect it to take a short time to see the basement collection, be sure to schedule LOTS of time; Rose will tell you endless details about his buildings, what they are made of, how he made them, what happened to the real structure, and so on, and so on until you, too, are an expert on all things Wakarusian.

325 S. Elkhart St., Wakarusa, IN 46573

(574) 862-2367

Hours: Monday–Friday 8 A.M.–5 P.M., Saturday 8 A.M.–noon

Cost: Adults $4, Kids $2

Directions: Three blocks south of Rte. 40.

WABASH
Wabash claims to be "The World's First Electrically Lighted City," because four arc lights were placed around the courthouse on March 31, 1880.

Singer **Crystal Gayle** (born Brenda Gail Webb) grew up in Wabash, graduating from Wabash High School in 1970. She was in the National Honor Society.

WHEATFIELD
By law, women may not wear halter tops, bathing suits, or short-shorts to political rallies in Wheatfield.

WHITING
The town of Whiting hosts its Pierogi Festival on the last full weekend of July each year. For details, call (877) 659-0292.

WINAMAC
The nationally watched 1980 trial regarding the 1973 Ford Pinto was held at the Pulaski County Courthouse (Main & Jefferson Sts.) in Winamac. Three local teens were killed in a gas tank fire, but Ford was found not guilty of reckless homicide after a 10-week trial.

Warsaw
Biblical Gardens

If you thought the Bible was only filled with "God said this" and "God said that," think again. It's also a botanical record of historic Middle Eastern plants—*holy* plants! Biblical Gardens claims to be America's largest collection of biblical flora with more than 80 species crammed into a plot smaller than an acre. A path winds through the flower beds, where small plaques indicate where you can find the species referenced in the holy book. Feel free to bring a picnic basket *and* your Bible to make a day of it. But be careful: if a serpent in a tree offers you an Apple of Knowledge, don't take it! To find out why, consult your Bible—it's somewhere near the beginning. . . .

Center Lake Park, Canal & N. Indiana Sts., Warsaw, IN 46580

(574) 267-6419

E-mail: peheimbach@warsawbiblicalgardens.com

Hours: April–October, dawn–dusk

Cost: Free

www.warsawbiblicalgardens.org

Directions: Just west of Detroit St. (Rte. 15), on the southeast corner of Warsaw Central Park, north of the McDonald's.

Hallmark Ornament Museum

The Party Shop would be just another knickknack and card emporium were it not for a large display in the back of the store. The Hallmark Ornament Museum is the collection of Jess Prudencio and David Hamrick, and it includes every Hallmark Keepsake Ornament produced since 1973, when the company started manufacturing them.

While they may be valuable to those who collect them, the early Keepsake Ornaments are extremely ugly—either dull balls with imprinted designs or hideous '70s yarn art, the kind your cat batted around, chewed up, and regurgitated years ago. In 1977, Hallmark branched out into fake stained glass, but they were no more interesting than the previous designs. Only when the company started making plastic figurines did things get interesting.

Were they not hung on a tree in December, it would be hard to figure out that many of these ornaments are Christmas decorations. You'll find such odd subjects as a bottle of Hershey's Syrup, a *Wheel of Fortune* wheel, the Jetsons in a Space Car, a coop full of singing chickens, Myra Gulch riding a bike (from *The Wizard of Oz*), a Scooby Doo thermos, and the starship *Enterprise*'s captains Kirk and Picard. The Party Shop has many of the old ornaments still for sale, so if you have your eye on that reindeer on a Jet Ski, it's yours . . . for a price.

The Party Shop, 3418 Lake City Highway, Warsaw, IN 46580

(800) 378-8694 or (574) 267-8787

Hours: Monday–Saturday 9:30 A.M.–9 P.M., Sunday noon–5 P.M.

Cost: Free

www.thepartyshop.com

Directions: In the K-Mart Shopping Center south of Rte. 30, at the east end of town.

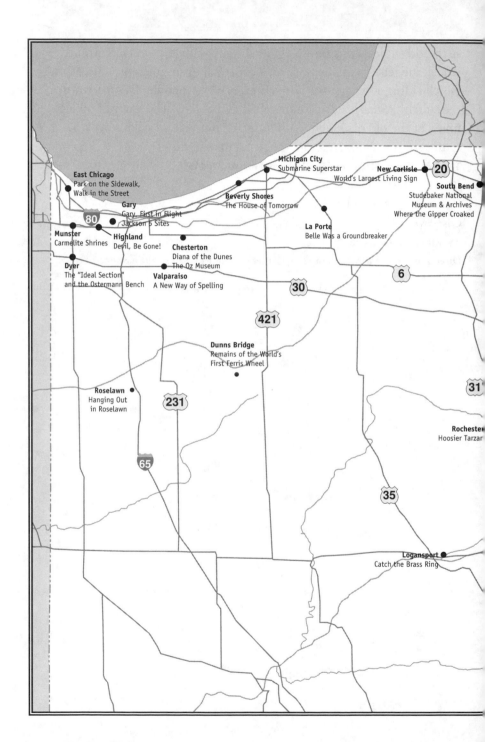

East Chicago
Park on the Sidewalk,
Walk in the Street

Gary
Gary, First in Flight
Jackson 5 Sites

Munster
Carmelite Shrines

Highland
Devil, Be Gone!

Dyer
The "Ideal Section"
and the Ostermann Bench

Chesterton
Diana of the Dunes
The Oz Museum

Valparaiso
A New Way of Spelling

Beverly Shores
The House of Tomorrow

Michigan City
Submarine Superstar

New Carlisle
World's Largest Living Sign

South Bend
Studebaker National
Museum & Archives
Where the Gipper Croaked

La Porte
Belle Was a Groundbreaker

Dunns Bridge
Remains of the World's
First Ferris Wheel

Roselawn
Hanging Out
in Roselawn

Rochester
Hoosier Tarzan

Logansport
Catch the Brass Ring

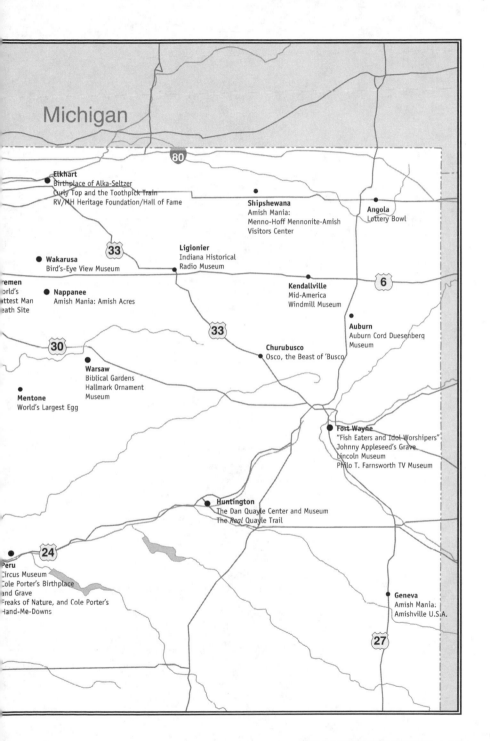

Michigan

80

Elkhart
Birthplace of Alka-Seltzer
Curly Top and the Toothpick Train
RV/MH Heritage Foundation/Hall of Fame

Shipshewana
Amish Mania:
Menno-Hoff Mennonite-Amish
Visitors Center

Angola
Lottery Bowl

33

Wakarusa
Bird's-Eye View Museum

Ligionier
Indiana Historical
Radio Museum

remen
orld's
attest Man
eath Site

Nappanee
Amish Mania: Amish Acres

Kendallville
Mid-America
Windmill Museum

6

Auburn
Auburn Cord Duesenberg
Museum

33

30

Churubusco
Osco, the Beast of 'Busco

Warsaw
Biblical Gardens
Hallmark Ornament
Museum

Mentone
World's Largest Egg

Fort Wayne
"Fish Eaters and Idol Worshipers"
Johnny Appleseed's Grave
Lincoln Museum
Philo T. Farnsworth TV Museum

Huntington
The Dan Quayle Center and Museum
The *Real* Quayle Trail

24

Peru
Circus Museum
Cole Porter's Birthplace
and Grave
Freaks of Nature, and Cole Porter's
Hand-Me-Downs

Geneva
Amish Mania:
Amishville U.S.A.

27

central INDiaNa

Central Indiana. Could anywhere be as "Middle America" as the middle region of the middle state in the Midwest? But just scratch beneath the surface of this region's practical, middle-class skin and you'll find these Hoosiers have cantankerous interiors, if for no other reason than to give the middle finger to their middle-of-the-road image.

Judge for yourself. Terre Haute is the only place in the universe where you can buy *square* donuts. When a tree began growing on the roof of the 10-story courthouse in Greensburg, citizens didn't chop it down—they pruned it. James Dean, David Letterman, and Jim Jones didn't launch their unconventional careers in California, but central Indiana. And one of the nation's oldest Spiritualist camps is located smack dab in the middle of it all.

Don't misunderstand—it's not like central Indiana folk are weirdoes. Heck, when the U.S. Air Force needed civilian volunteers to sit in an isolated watch tower and watch for incoming Soviet aircraft, almost a hundred Lafayette area residents said, "Sign me up!" They know when it's time to get serious. Still, you never know when you'll bump into a giant sneaker, a squirrel-cage jail, or a green-eyed concrete dog.

Alamo
America's Least-Dead Revolutionary Soldier

When George Fruits died in 1876, it marked the end of a generation of soldiers. Fruits (some say his name was Fruts) was the last surviving veteran of the Revolutionary War. He had served with the Pennsylvania militia, and passed on at the ripe old age of 114.

You do the math—he was only 14 when the war broke out. Still a teenager when the conflict ended, he had a lot of life left in him. He eventually married Catherine Stonebraker, who was many years younger than George. The couple moved west in 1820, and were two of this region's first settlers. When Fruits died, Catherine finally, *finally*, was able to start drawing a widow's pension.

Stonebraker Cemetery, County Road 400S, Alamo, IN 47916

No phone

Hours: Daylight hours

Cost: Free

Directions: Half a mile west of Country Rd. 600W.

ANDERSON

A mysterious dead eight-inch squid was discovered in the sludge pits of Anderson's Delphi Interior and Lighting Systems Plant 9 (2401 Columbus Ave.) on November 15, 1996. The pits, filled with oil, stripper, antifreeze, and polyal were not conducive to most life forms.

An Anderson man was "scanned" by a mysterious light he believed came from a UFO on August 12, 1981. He was standing in a field watching a meteor shower when it happened.

BRAZIL

Orville Redenbacher was born in Brazil on July 16, 1907.

Jimmy Hoffa was born at 103 N. Vandalia Street in Brazil on February 14, 1913. The doctor who delivered him thought Hoffa's mother had a tumor, not a baby, in her abdomen. During his early years, he was referred to as "The Tumor."

Nobody messes with Nancy Barnett!

Amity
Nancy Barnett Isn't Moving!

In 1831, long before the first automobile was invented in Kokomo, Nancy Kerlin Barnett was buried in a small cemetery along the banks of Sugar Creek. She rested in peace for about 70 years before the modern world began knocking on her door. County officials were planning a road and determined that the best route followed a trail that cut through the center of Barnett's cemetery.

This obstacle didn't bother the engineers; they just began moving the bodies to another location. But it did bother Barnett's grandson, Daniel Doty. Though he was born 15 years after Barnett died, he felt an obligation to protect her grave—by force if necessary. So, while the exhumations continued, he sat atop her mound with a gun across his lap. Doty was still there when the road crew laid a gravel bed on either side of her plot, and when the road was finished, he had one more job left to do. In 1912, he saw that a concrete slab was placed atop her grave to protect her from those who might not notice the rather significant speed bump in the center median. You'll still find Nancy there today.

Hill's Camp Road, Amity, IN 46131

No phone

Hours: Always visible

Cost: Free

Directions: South from Amity on Rte. 31, turn east on County Rd. 400S and follow it past Sugar Creek.

Battle Ground
Tippecanoe Battlefield Monument

William Henry Harrison got a lot of political mileage from a battle that took place just north of Lafayette on November 7, 1811. His military victory at the Battle of Tippecanoe was made possible, in part, by the idiotic advice given to his foe, Tecumseh, by his one-eyed brother Tenskwatawa, better known as The Prophet.

It was like Jimmy Carter taking military advice from Billy. Just before his fateful conflict with Harrison's invading militia, The Prophet (a medicine man) claimed to have had visions of the invading army's musket balls passing right through his followers' bodies without harming them. And he was half right.

Clad in little more than The Prophet's assurances, the warriors made a preemptive strike against Harrison's encampment of 1,000 men, killing a total of 68 officers and men, but they suffered greater casualties than they inflicted. Fleeing the battle, the Native American survivors wanted to kill The Prophet, but settled for a curse Tecumseh supposedly inflicted on the U.S. government for provoking this conflict: He claimed that every president elected in a year ending in zero would die in office. (Before this, no American president had died while serving.)

James Monroe was elected in 1820 and lived out his term. So much for the curse. But in 1840, William Henry Harrison—remember him?—campaigning under a mocking, to-hell-with-the-Indian-curse slogan "Tippecanoe and Tyler, too!", was elevated to the nation's highest office . . . and dropped dead 31 days later. Harrison had caught pneumonia while giving his inaugural address. Then Abraham Lincoln, first elected in 1860, was assassinated. James A. Garfield (victor in 1880) was also gunned down, as was William McKinley, whose second term began in 1900. Warren Harding, the 1920 winner, died in office three years later, possibly at the hands of his wife. FDR was reelected for a second time in 1940 and perished after his third reelection. John Kennedy? Everyone knows what happened to the 1960 winner . . . or thinks they do. Ronald Reagan may have broken the string, but not without getting a bullet in the chest. George W. Bush is the most recent chief executive to flaunt Tecumseh's presidential curse.

200 Battleground Ave., Battle Ground, IN 47920

(765) 567-2147

Hours: March–November, daily 10 A.M.–5 P.M.; December–February 10 A.M.–4 P.M.

Cost: Battlefield, Free; Museum, Adults $3, Seniors (60+) $2, Kids (4–12) $2

www.tcha.mus.in.us/battlefield.htm

Directions: South of town on 9th Rd. to Battleground Ave.

Wolf Park

Ignoring advice from the Three Little Pigs and Little Red Riding Hood, a wolf sanctuary has been established in the American heartland. The folks at Wolf Park believe the lovable lupines have gotten a bad rap and, given the informative presentations at this nature center, they might be right.

The wolves here are not allowed to hang around and wait for a sirloin handout, but must work for their food. Friday and Saturday evenings are Howl Nights where the wolves sing for their supper. On Sunday afternoons, the pack is encouraged to develop their tracking and hunting skills on a herd of penned bison. You're invited to all the demonstrations, and all the proceeds go to preserve this endangered species.

4012 E. County Road 800N, Battle Ground, IN 47920

(765) 567-2265

Hours: May–November, Tuesday–Sunday 1–5 P.M.; Wolf Howl Nights, May–November, Friday–Saturday 7:30 P.M.; December–April, Saturday 7:30 P.M.

Cost: Adults $4, Kids (6–13) $3

www.wolfpark.org

Directions: Head east out of Battle Ground on Rte. 225, turn north on Jefferson St., look for sign to Wolf Park 1.5 miles north.

No, no, no. The wrenches go on the *inside*.

Bryant
A Wrenching Barn

If you're like most people, you lose more tools than you find. Blame your neighbor. Blame the kids. Blame your own laziness and lack of organization. Or blame the owner of this barn in Bryant, who's located at the other end of the universe's tool wormhole. When wrenches disappear in your world, they turn up here. Hundreds of wrenches have appeared over the years, and they now hang on the outside of this structure.

Each wrench has been painted bright yellow to make it visible to passersby. If you see a tool that disappeared from your garage years ago, do you think you'll be able to get it back? Not on your life; they're firmly wired to the walls, so don't even try it!

Hardly Able Ranch, Route 27 & Elm St., Bryant, IN 47326

No phone

Hours: Always visible

Cost: Free

Directions: On the west side of the road, just south of Rtes. 27 and 67.

Let's see the Russkies get past THIS!

Cairo
Eyes to the Skies!

The Russians were coming! The Russians were coming! . . . Or so the folks of Cairo were led to believe. Before the military was able to install a national radar system, the U.S. Air Force came up with a low-tech solution: Operation Skywatch. Patriotic citizens were asked to volunteer to sit in watch towers all across the nation and keep their eyes and ears peeled for enemy aircraft. They were known as the Civilian Ground Observation Corps.

The Cairo Tower, also known as Delta Lima 3-Green, was commissioned on August 16, 1952, and staffed by a group of 90 volunteers on rotating shifts. It was the first Operation Skywatch tower in the nation. Perhaps the Air Force thought it best to start in the center of the country and work its way out.

Today the tower stands empty, its stairs collapsing, while a vigilant limestone statue of a *Leave It to Beaver* family gazes skyward. A plaque reads, "They also serve who stand and watch." So true.

County Road 850N, Cairo, IN 47923

No phone

Hours: Always visible

Cost: Free

Directions: Just east of County Road 100W on County Road 850N in the center of town, just south of the I-65 overpass.

Chesterfield
Spiritualist Camp

Long before there were telephone psychics, spiritualists were the folks people turned to for answers to otherworldly questions. So what is spiritualism? According to this place's literature, it's "the Science, Philosophy, and Religion of continuous life, based on the fact of communication, by means of mediumship, with those who live in the spirit world." Translation? If you pony up the dough, we'll help you talk to your dead aunt.

This Spiritualist camp was founded by Dr. J. Westerfield in 1890. During the years following the Civil War, spiritualism was very popular with Americans who wanted to contact loved ones lost in battle. The practice of contacting the dead suffered a tremendous setback when the Fox sisters, who singlehandedly started the movement, confessed that they were not receiving "raps" from beyond the grave, but were popping bones in their feet in answer to questions.

That didn't stop the true believers. Spiritualism survives to this day in a few places around the country, like Chesterfield. Built as a sort of "medium's commune," with small huts surrounding a central park, you can pick up a listing of those accepting clients at the main office. On a nice day, the mediums sit out on their porches, waiting for business with their prices clearly posted. To avoid a price war, all have agreed to standard fees: $30 for a 30-minute Private Clairvoyance or Healing, $35 for a Private Trumpet or Trance, etc. You can save money by arranging for a larger group in a séance, but you'll have to share your communication with your departed Aunt Clara.

The grounds of the camp are filled with statues, totem poles, and creepy moss-covered benches. If you call ahead, you can have them unlock the Hett Art Gallery and Museum. It's filled with paintings rendered while channeling spirits through an artist's brush strokes.

Camp Chesterfield, 225 Western Dr., PO Box 132, Chesterfield, IN 46017

(765) 378-0235

Hours: Daily 9 A.M.–5 P.M.; call ahead for church services or to see the museum

Cost: Free; seances extra

www.campchesterfield.net

Directions: Off Rte. 32 in the center of town, two blocks north of the Rte. 232 intersection.

Cicero
Ryan White's Real Hometown and Grave

The difference between what Ryan White's family experienced in Kokomo and how folks welcomed them in Cicero could not be more stark. He was immediately befriended by the student body president of Hamilton Heights High School (25802 Route 19, Arcadia), Jill Stewart, and other neighbors. Hamilton Heights had already launched an AIDS education program at the school in anticipation of White's arrival. With a new red Mustang, given to him by Michael Jackson, Ryan was a celebrity at his new school. He admitted in his memoirs that the local police never wrote him any speeding tickets, though he was pulled over several times. Leadfoots today are not offered the same courtesy.

During the summer months, White acted as an extra in a movie about his life and got a job at a local mall. The virus eventually caught up with him, and on April 8, 1990, Palm Sunday, White died at Riley Children's Hospital (702 Barnhill Dr., Indianapolis). Services were held at the Second Presbyterian Church (7700 N. Meridian, Indianapolis) on April 11. White's pall bearers included Howie Long, Phil Donahue, and Elton John, and he was laid to rest in his real home town of Cicero beneath a large granite memorial.

Cicero Cemetery, 236th St. & Tollgate Rd., Cicero, IN 46034

No phone

Hours: Daily 9 A.M.–6 P.M.

Cost: Free

Directions: West of Rte. 19 on 236th St., at the west end of town, on the south side of the road.

Cloverdale
House of Bells

Some in the community of Cloverdale might think the Kennedy family are a bunch of dingdongs, to which the Kennedys might reply, "Thank you very much!" While most folks are satisfied with a lawn gnome or two, the Kennedys have filled their rural yard with bells, bells, and more bells. They call it the Texas Mouse Trap, and it includes some nonringing items, such as windmills, anchor chains, giant axes, and large bear traps. You'd think noise would be a problem for the neighbors, but the Kennedys live way out in the country and can clang away to their hearts' desires.

4291 County Road 900E, Cloverdale, IN 46120

Private phone

Hours: Always visible

Cost: Free

Directions: West of town five miles on Rte. 42, turn right on County Rd. 900E when Rte. 42 makes a sharp turn north at the county line.

CLIFTON
A shower of brown worms fell on the town of Clifton in February 1892.

CONNORSVILLE
A UFO with a silver shell and three green doors was spotted by Terry Eversole and his sister near Connersville on October 11, 1973.

CRAWFORDSVILLE
Two icemen, Methodist pastor G. W. Switzer, and his wife spotted a 20-foot headless serpent moving through the sky propelled by "fin-like attachments" on September 5, 1891, near Crawfordsville. It returned two nights later to terrorize a crowd of frightened onlookers.

DANA
War correspondent **Ernie Pyle** was born outside Dana on August 3, 1900. His birth home has been moved to town and converted to a museum [120 Briarwood St., (765) 665-3633].

Crawfordsville
Ben Hur Museum
When you think of Ben Hur, you probably think of Rome. Or chariot races. Or Charlton Heston's overacting. But do you ever think of *Crawfordsville, Indiana*? You should, for it was here that the book was written, under a beech tree near the Hoosier home of Major General Lew Wallace.

Wallace was a soldier, an artist, a violinist, an inventor, and a territorial governor of New Mexico; but he will be remembered most for writing *Ben Hur*, first published in 1880. The book was a hit even before it landed on the silver screen. Wallace's study is surrounded by a frieze depicting the exploits of his heroic character, and you'll also find two costumes from Hollywood's interpretations of his tale. A statue of Wallace stands on the museum grounds. Each October the town of Crawfordsville holds a chariot race to honor its man of letters.

Wallace was born in downstate Brookville on April 10, 1827. When he died in Crawfordsville in 1906, he was buried in Oak Hill Cemetery.

Lew Wallace Study, 501 W. Pike St., Crawfordsville, IN 47933

(765) 362-5769

E-mail: study@wico.net

Hours: April–May, September–October, Tuesday–Sunday 1–4:30 P.M.; June–August, Tuesday 1–4:30 P.M., Wednesday–Saturday 10 A.M.–4:30 P.M., Sunday 1–4:30 P.M.; March and November, Saturday–Sunday 1–4:30 P.M.

Cost: Adults $3, Kids (6–12) $1

www.ben-hur.com

Directions: At the corner of Pike St. & Wallace Ave.

Oak Hill Cemetery, 598 Oak Hill Rd., Crawfordsville, IN 47933

(765) 362-6602

Hours: Daily 9 A.M.–5 P.M.

Cost: Free

Directions: Head north on Rte. 231 from downtown, over the bridge; Oak Hill Rd. is the first main road leading west.

Old Jail Museum
Round and round the criminals go, and where they stop determines if they go. Welcome to the Montgomery County Jail, the world's first circular, rotating jail.

Construction on the unique building was started in 1881 and completed a year later. It was the brainchild of William H. Brown and Benjamin F. Haugh, intended as a means of reducing the number of law enforcement officials needed to guard a jailful of ne'er-do-wells. The concept was simple: build a two-story set of 16 cells, each cell shaped like a wedge, that could be turned by an external crank. This oversized coffee can rotated within another set of bars, this one with a single exit. Spin an interior cell's door to match with the external door, and the inmate could go in or out. All the rest would have to wait.

This design had obvious drawbacks, particularly in a fire, but this didn't concern the county much and they continued to use it from 1882 until 1939. At that time, the drum was welded to keep it from rotating, and multiple doors were cut into the outer cage. This stationary jail was used until 1973. Eventually, the structure was put on the National Register of Historic Places and restored. Every September the town throws a Labor Day Breakout where folks get the rare opportunity to see the jail turn.

225 N. Washington St., Crawfordsville, IN 47933

(765) 362-5222

Hours: June–August, Wednesday–Saturday 10 a.m.–4:30 p.m., Tuesday and Sunday 1–4:30 p.m.; April–May and September–October, Wednesday–Sunday 1:30–4:30 p.m.

Cost: Free

www.crawfordsville.org/jail/

Directions: On Rte. 231 (Washington St.) just north of Rte. 136.

Crete & Lynn
Jim Jones, That Lovable Tyke!

Everyone's got to start somewhere, and for the Reverend Jim Jones, that somewhere was the dinky town of Crete near the Indiana–Ohio border. He was born on May 13, 1931, to Jim and Lynetta Jones, both of whom would help launch young Jim on the road to kookdom. Lynetta believed she was the reincarnation of Mark Twain, and told family and friends that her departed mother had come to her in a dream to proclaim she would give birth to the World's Savior. Talk about pressure!

Jones's father worked for the railroad, if "worked" meant "collected a paycheck." For the better part of his life he was plagued by alcoholism and depression, and not without reason—he returned home from World War

I with his lungs nearly destroyed by mustard gas. The elder Jones spent his free hours at the local watering holes, wheezing out war stories with the local drunks. He was also a member of the local KKK.

Jones Birthplace, 8400 S. Arba Pike, Crete, IN 47355

Private phone

Hours: Private property; view from street

Cost: Free

Directions: The first house on the right, heading south from Rte. 36 along Arba Pike.

Everyone's got to start somewhere.

Luckily for Crete, the family didn't stay long after the railroad rerouted through Lynn in 1934. The family moved into a small house along the tracks on the south side of town. Little Jim became known as Lynn's version of St. Francis, always followed by a collection of stray dogs, cats, and other critters. At first he was content to let them run free, but soon he built cages for his menagerie in the family barn. Was this a sign of things to come?

Residents recalled how little Jim liked to run around naked, or at least pantless, until it was time to enter school. He could also be coaxed to deliver profanity-filled diatribes for a five-cent gratuity. The local trouble-makers always had a spare nickel for the kid who cursed on command.

Early on, Jones attended religious services with his family at the tame Church of the Nazarene (425 S. Main St.). But soon he began attending a Holy Roller congregation on the west side of Lynn, the Gospel Tabernacle, where they spoke in tongues and actually stood up in the pews. The minister soon capitalized on Jim's swearing talent, turning his foulmouthed rants-for-pay into fire-and-brimstone sermons from the new child preacher.

Outside church, Jim would baptize his friends in a nearby creek and preside over funerals for rats and other dead animals. When most kids might play cowboys and Indians, Jim set up an altar in the barn and would preach to his playmates, attracting his "congregation" with lemon-ade and punch during the hot summer months. (Another omen?) While it didn't seem too odd at the time, he once locked his friends in the loft when they threatened to leave his group. That wacky kid!

He also had a passion for science, and converted the barn into a labo-ratory between services. Jones would set up a microscope with insect specimens, or perform experiments, like the time he tried to graft a chicken leg onto a duck with string. Sometimes he would combine sci-ence and religion, reviving supposedly ailing rabbits and chickens. Jim was also his own biological oddity; childhood friends said he could, while standing on the ground, piss almost to the peak of the barn. (This once passed for entertainment in Lynn.)

The Jones home, barn, and outhouse are long gone, replaced by a small supermarket. The Gospel Tabernacle, where Jones first preached, is today used as an office for Kabert Industries.

Thornburg's Supermarket, 202 S. Main St., Lynn, IN 47355

(765) 874-2325

Hours: Home torn down

Cost: Free

Directions: At the corner of Grant & Main St. (Rte. 27), south of Church St.

Kabert Industries, 511 W. Church St., Lynn, IN 47355

Private phone

Hours: Always visible; view from street

Cost: Free

Directions: Five blocks west of Main St. (Rte. 27).

Fairmount
James Dean's Boyhood Home

Few Hoosiers have left as big an impression on the outside world as James Dean, and no community in the state has gotten as much mileage out of this long-dead rebel as Fairmount, the town in which he grew up.

Dean was born in nearby Marion (see p. 91), but his family moved to California when he was an infant. After his mother died of cancer, his father sent the nine-year-old back to Indiana to live on the farm of Ortense and Marcus Winslow, Jimmy's aunt and uncle. The family attended the Back Creek Friends Church and Jimmy was enrolled at West Ward Elementary, also known as "Old Academy."

There aren't too many stories about Dean's childhood, mostly because his life at the time was typical and uneventful: Jimmy did his chores, obeyed the Winslows, and played a lot with his young cousin Marcus. Dean knocked out four front teeth while playing in the Winslows' barn (which still stands), and learned to play basketball with a basket "hoop" nailed up by his uncle.

After his death, the Winslows were initially very open to talking to visitors, at least until they loaned a family photo album to a "reporter" doing a story on their famous nephew. It has never been returned. The farm is still owned by the family, Dean's cousin Marcus to be exact.

7184 County Road 150E, Jonesboro, IN 46938

Private phone

Hours: Always visible

Cost: Free

www.jdean.com

Directions: Drive north past the cemetery on County Rd. 150E, on the west side of the road, just past County Rd. 700S.

Fairmount High School

In high school, James Dean began exhibiting the personal traits and tastes that would become his trademark. After Dean gave a rousing monologue for the school's annual Women's Christian Temperance Union competition, drama coach Adeline Nall invited him to participate in the school plays, a request she did not regret—even when he fired a gun into the set wall to give it a look of realism for a mystery play. (Dean later said of Nall, "That chick was a frustrated actress.") His first acting lessons took place in Room 21 of the now crumbling building. He was cast in *You Can't Take It with You, Our Hearts Were Young and Gay, Mooncalf Mungford, The Monkey's Paw,* and *Goon With the Wind* as Frankenstein.

Though Dean was a Quaker and theoretically nonviolent, he was not above getting into scrapes. He was suspended for punching schoolmate Dave Fox for criticizing his reasoning during a debate class.

Dean owned a motorcycle and he rode everywhere, spending a lot of time at Marvin Carter's motorcycle shop (just north of the cemetery on County Road 150E). Once, at the Jonesboro High School baseball park, Dean accepted a dare from two young women to ride his motorcycle nude with friend Clyde Smitson; when the naked pair returned to the park the women had run off with their clothes, so they had to drive back to Fairmount au naturel.

During high school, Jimmy established a close relationship with Methodist minister James DeWeerd, who taught him yoga, showed him his travel movies, told him about bullfighting, and encouraged him to sculpt. The Reverend DeWeerd also taught Dean to drive and took him to the Indy 500, where the teenager got his first look at real speed. In retrospect, this might not have been the best lesson.

James Dean graduated May 16, 1949, and left for California two weeks later. His old high school stands empty and is in danger of being torn down. Fairmount boosters are doing all they can to keep it from a date with a wrecking ball.

Old Fairmount High School, Jefferson & Vine Sts., Fairmount, IN 46928

No phone

Hours: Always visible

Cost: Free

Directions: From Main and Washington, go three blocks east and two blocks south.

FAIRMOUNT
The town of Fairmount used to be called Pucker.

Rebel Not Without a Following.

James Dean's Grave

Following his fatal accident on September 30, 1955, Dean's body was returned to Fairmount for burial. Some (including Walter Winchell) had rumored aloud that Dean was alive but maimed, and was learning to use his artificial limbs before returning to society. Services were held at the Friends Church (124 W. First St.) on October 8. James DeWeerd gave the eulogy.

Dean's grave in Park Cemetery is an ever-changing monument. Shortly after his burial, a brick monument was erected in the cemetery with a bust of the star, but the statue soon disappeared. At first fans were suspected, but later evidence revealed that it was sawed off by a local veterans' group who thought Dean had improperly avoided the draft by claiming he was gay. "I kissed the doctor!" he told Hedda Hopper. (In reality, Dean was telling half the truth; he was bisexual.) Hopper later lobbied to have a granite Oscar awarded posthumously to Dean, to be placed on his grave. It never happened.

Dean's first headstone disappeared for eight years, then reappeared. It was stolen again in 1983, but when it didn't return it was replaced in 1985. Eventually, the first marker showed up behind a Fort Wayne dumpster in 1987. The second Dean headstone was taken on June 14, 1998, but found two days later by a sheriff's deputy after he ran over it on a country road 60 miles away.

Though chipped and battered, the Dean marker is usually surrounded by flowers, coated in lipstick prints, and covered in items from fans. Packs of Chesterfield cigarettes are a popular offering. Remember, this is a cemetery, so visitors are asked to show some respect. Leaving mementos is fine; wailing and throwing yourself on the grave is not.

Park Cemetery, Route 150, Fairmount, IN 46928

(765) 948-4040

Hours: Daily 9 A.M.–6 P.M.

Cost: Free

Directions: North on Main (Rte. 150) heading out of town, on the left.

Fairmount Historical Museum

Dean fans will find plenty in Fairmount to keep them busy, including two museums. The first is run by the local historical society, and includes plenty of items not associated with the town's favorite son.

The Fairmount Historical Museum has an impressive collection of Dean artifacts, most donated by his family and friends. (The museum is housed in the J. W. Patterson home, built by Nixon Winslow, James Dean's great-grandfather.) Dean's first Fairmount motorcycle was discovered in downstate Indiana, restored, and is now parked back here under glass. They've got his conga drums, a yellow sweater left unclaimed at Del Mar Cleaners after his death, the boots he wore in *Giant*, his grammar school art, and a soil experiment from 4H.

The museum sponsors the annual Museum Days Celebration on the last weekend in September. Dean fans from across the nation descend on the small town for a street fair, classic car rally, look-alike contest, free screenings of Dean's three films, and much more.

203 E. Washington, PO Box 92, Fairmount, IN 46928

(317) 948-4555

Hours: March–November, Monday–Saturday 10 A.M.–5 P.M., Sunday noon–5 P.M.

Cost: Adults $1 donation

Directions: Downtown, one block east of Main St. on Washington St. (County Rd. 950S).

James Dean Memorial Gallery

James Dean's former acting teacher, Adeline Nall, used a switchblade to cut the ribbon at the opening of the James Dean Gallery several years back, and this fan museum has been busy ever since. The gallery is filled with Dean-abilia; most of the souvenirs and trinkets were produced after his death. But they also have many genuine items on display, including a "life mask" created for makeup artists on his films, 12 pieces of clothing he wore in his brief movie career (including the wool pants he wore during the *Rebel Without a Cause* knife fight and an outfit from *East of Eden*), old posters, high school yearbooks, artworks the actor created, and lots and lots of bad art created by his fans. There seems to be a universal error in the pieces: Dean's head always looks too large for his body.

The James Dean Gallery has the best gift shop in town. You name it, his brooding image is plastered on it—mugs, ties, magnets, statuettes, plates, puzzles, Christmas ornaments—nothing is too uncool for the man who invented cool.

425 N. Main St., Fairmount, IN 46928

(765) 948-DEAN (948-3326)

Hours: Daily 9 A.M.–6 P.M.

Cost: Adults $3.75

www.JamesDeanGallery.com

Directions: Four blocks south of Rte. 26 on Main St.

AND THAT'S NOT ALL!

Gaze up at the Fairmount water tower and you'll see not only James Dean, but Garfield the Cat. Why? Cartoonist **Jim Davis** grew up just outside of town, off Route 26, on a 120-acre farm with 25 cats.

It turns out that Fairmount has been the hometown of many celebrities, and claims to have 14 times the national average of entries in *Who's Who*, per capita. There's CBS correspondent **Phil Jones**. And **Cyrus Pemberton**, creator of the ice cream cone in 1904. And **Bill Dolman**, hamburger inventor. And **Milton Wright**, the father of the Wright Brothers. Who knows who the gene pool will come up with next!??

Fountain City
Grand Central Station on the Underground Railroad

Between 1827 and 1847 (at this site, and before they lived here), Levi and Catharine Coffin helped more than 2,000 slaves escape to freedom in the North, and because of this Fountain City earned the designation of "Grand Central Station on the Underground Railroad." Not one slave who passed through this station during those 20 years was ever lost to the slave trade. In that respect, the Coffins had a *better* track record than Grand Central Station.

Levi Coffin was unofficially dubbed the president of the movement. The Coffins were the inspiration for Harriet Beecher Stowe's Simeon and Rachel Halliday in *Uncle Tom's Cabin*, and the story of one of their real "passengers," Eliza Harris, became the fictitious "Eliza," who escaped across an Ohio River ice floe with her baby in her arms.

The Coffins' home has been restored to its antebellum appearance with period furnishings. On the tour, you will see the hiding place in the attic located behind the headboard, and another between the mattresses on the bed.

Levi Coffin House State Historic Park, 113 N. Main St., PO Box 77, Fountain City, IN 47341

(765) 847-2432

Hours: June–August, Tuesday–Saturday 1–4 P.M.; September–October, Saturday 1–4 P.M.

Cost: Adults $2, Kids (6–18) $1

www.waynet.org/nonprofit/coffin.htm

Directions: Where Main St. (Rte. 27) meets Fountain City Pike.

FRANKFORT

Each year in July Frankfort holds a Hot Dog Festival. The high school's mascot is the Fighting Hot Dog.

Will "Grampa Walton" **Geer** was born in Frankfort on March 9, 1902.

Skip this site if you're from London . . .

Greencastle
Buzz Bomb

It was the terror of London, the German V-1 buzz bomb. During Axis attacks in the later years of World War II, Britons were familiar with the sound of the first guided missiles' engines buzzing overhead. As long as they could hear sound, folks on the ground were safe, but when the noise cut off the V-1s returned to earth.

The V-1 that now sits on the courthouse lawn in Greencastle was decommissioned by the army, purchased by locals just after the war, and dedicated to local veterans on Memorial Day 1947. Would those veterans have felt differently had they been British soldiers? Bloody likely!

Putnam County Courthouse, 1 Court House Square, Greencastle, IN 46135

No phone

Hours: Always visible

Cost: Free

Directions: On the southwest corner of the courthouse, along Rte. 231, at the corner of Washington and Jackson Sts.

Dan Quayle's Frat House

Described by writer Gail Sheehy as "a hotbed for social rest" during the 1960s, DePauw University was the perfect place for Dan Quayle's undergraduate career. His father claimed Dan majored in "booze and broads." Not true, said Quayle classmate Joseph Wert; Quayle majored in "girls, golf, and alcohol." Wow—a triple major!

Not surprisingly, Quayle pledged a fraternity at DePauw: Delta Kappa Epsilon, better known as the Dekes. This was the same house pledged by both George Bushes at Yale. His nickname was sometimes "Skippy," for his boyish enthusiasm for childish behavior; and some-times "Faceman," for his supposed good looks. Fraternity brother Clark Adams claimed Quayle "was not a guy to take a position on anything except who his date was on Friday night and where to get drunk on Saturday night."

After four years of hard work, Quayle walked away with a 2.16 grade point average. One of his former English professors, William Cavanaugh, summed it up: "Behind those big blue eyes there was nothing." Perhaps that's why, when the university wanted to give Quayle an honorary degree in 1982, the faculty overturned its request. The college's president trumped his staff and awarded Quayle the unearned degree anyway.

The Deke chapter at DePauw is no longer active, but the old frat house is still there.

Delta Kappa Epsilon House, Psi Phi Chapter, 620 E. Anderson, Greencastle, IN 46135

Hours: Always visible; no longer active

Cost: Free

www.dke.org

Directions: Two blocks south of Rte 240 and Rte. 231 intersection, off Rte. 231 heading east in Anderson; room on the third floor, above the balcony on the left.

Greenfield & St. Leon
The Old Crow and the Hickory Pole

If you think the nation's recent presidential election was strange, you should hear how things used to be. Two little-known customs can be traced back to the Hoosier State.

Before the donkey became the symbol of the Democratic Party, it was the rooster. It all began when Greenfield Democrat Joseph Chapman was asked to "crow up" support for William Henry Harrison in the 1840 election, and "Crow, Chapman, crow!" became a rallying cry. The rooster remained the Democratic mascot for years, until the party switched to a donkey. You can find a monument to Chapman's first squawk at the entrance to Riley Memorial Park in his old home town.

Riley Memorial Park, E. Main St. & West Dr., Greenfield, IN 46140

No phone

Hours: Always visible

Cost: Free

Directions: Eight blocks east of Rte. 9 on Main St. (Rte. 40)

Another strange tradition began four years later in 1844, when Democrats around the United States erected hickory poles in honor of former president Andrew "Old Hickory" Jackson. For many years, in an election year, it was common for towns to do the same. Somehow St. Leon got into the act in 1892, 55 years after Jackson was dead and buried, by erecting its first hickory pole in front of St. Joe's Church. It was hoisted by hand, and topped by an American flag and a fake rooster.

Whether they feel they're making up for all those lost years, or whether they're suckers for tradition, St. Leon is the only community in the nation that still raises a hickory pole every four years. And why doesn't anyone else still do this? Because it's ridiculous, that's why.

St. Joseph's Church, Church Lane, St. Leon, IN 47012

No phone

Hours: Always visible

Cost: Free

Directions: On the west side of the church.

This is what happens when you don't clean your gutters.

Greensburg
Tree on the Courthouse

This is what happens when you don't clean your gutters . . . for 130 years.
In 1870, caretakers (to use the term loosely) of the 1860 Decatur County
courthouse in Greensburg noticed a small tree had sprouted in a gutter
along the highest roof. They decided to let it grow, for curiosity's sake.
Over time, the large-tooth aspen grew big enough to see from the ground,
10 stories below. It grew, and grew, and grew, until it started to rip the
roof off the building.

Maintenance crews finally chopped down the 12-foot tree in 1919, but that didn't put an end to it. A "sucker" sprouted from the original tree's roots, and Greensburg mascot was back in business. Since then, a series of trees have either been reluctantly removed (when they grew too large) or blown off in windstorms. Remarkably, a new tree always returned.

Today's tree is the twelfth generation, having sprouted in 1958. Greensburg calls itself the "Tree City" and throws a festival each September to honor its out-of-place arboretum. Rest assured, if the suckers don't keep coming back in the gutters, the suckers on the ground will plant a new tree.

Courthouse Tower, 150 Courthouse Square, Greensburg, IN 47240

(812) 663-2832

Hours: Always visible

Cost: Free

www.greensburgchamber.com/tree%20history.html

Directions: At the corner of Broadway and Washington St. (Rte. 421).

Knightstown
William Arnold, Truck Stop Artist

Looking for art in a truck stop is like looking for motor oil at the Guggenheim—it just doesn't seem to make much sense. But the Gas America Truck Stop north of I-70 in Knightstown is an exception to the rule. Scattered around the pumps and parking lot are several animal sculptures made of intricately tangled wire. They're the creations of artist William Arnold, and if you'd like to meet him, he's usually at his Wire America studio just north of the minimart.

Tell Arnold what you want and he'll make it, from wildlife to human figures. Be patient; his reputation has him sitting on a backlog of two years' worth of orders. Pieces range anywhere from life-sized cardinals to eagles with 20-foot wingspans.

Gas American Truck Stop, I-70 & Rte. 109, Knightstown, IN 46148

Contact: Wire America, PO Box 357, Wilkinson, IN 46186

(765) 785-6747

E-mail: william@wiresoul.com

Hours: Call ahead

Cost: Free

www.wiresoul.com

Directions: Just north of the Rte. 109 exit from I-70.

CITY OF FIRSTS

For most towns, it might be enough to claim the world's first automobile, but not go-go-Kokomo, "The City of Firsts." No fewer than 15 earthshaking inventions were introduced in this town. (If there are any new ones, you can be sure to find them at members.iquest.net/~deglen/kokfirst.html)

Automobile (Elwood Haynes, 1894)

Pneumatic Rubber Tire (D. C. Spraker, 1894)

Aluminum Casting (Billy Johnson, 1895)

Carburetor (George Kingston, 1902)

Stainless Steel (Elwood Haynes, 1912)

Howitzer Shell (Superior Machine Tool Company, 1918)

Aerial Bomb with Fins (Liberty Pressed Metal, 1918)

Mechanical Corn Picker (John Powell, 1922)

Dirilyte Golden-Hued Tableware (Carl Molin, 1926)

Canned Tomato Juice (Kemp Brothers Canning, 1928)

Push-Button Car Radio (Delco, 1938)

All-Metal Lifeboat (Globe American Stove, 1941)

Signal-Seeking Car Radio (Delco, 1947)

Transistor Car Radio (Delco, 1957)

Kokomo and Russiaville
Ryan White, Pariah

If anyone needs a lesson in courage, they need look no further than the life of Ryan White. He was born in Kokomo on December 6, 1971, and named after Ryan O'Neal in *Love Story*. Doctors soon learned he suffered from hemophilia, the genetic disease that prevents blood from clotting. With blood-derived clotting factor, hemophiliacs can lead relatively average lives, which is what White was doing until the early 1980s when the AIDS epidemic began sweeping the globe. Doctors believe he contracted the virus from a blood transfusion in 1984.

As if his medical challenges weren't enough, the pain he suffered at the hands of the local community was far worse. Restaurants would throw out his plates and silverware after he'd eaten at their establishments. Customers would march out at the sight of him. Garbage was dumped on the family's lawn. The pastor at the St. Luke's United Methodist Church asked that Ryan sit in the first or last pew. Other ministers claimed Ryan was infected because his family weren't "good Christians," and Jerry Falwell charged Ryan's mother, Jeane White, with being an opportunistic grandstander—something he knew all about. Kids flattened themselves against the lockers when he walked by in the hallways. Adults accused him of biting other kids and spitting on vegetables at local grocery stores.

Through it all, Ryan White maintained a remarkably positive attitude, but when the local school district tried to get him banned from the classroom, the Whites fought back. At first Ryan was made to stay at home and attend classes through a telephone hookup. It barely worked. In an attempt to bolster their case for excluding him, the school board could find only one doctor willing to side with them, the personal physician of political nut-case Lyndon LaRouche.

In an agreement between both sides, White was allowed to return on February 21, 1986, if he agreed to skip gym, eat from paper plates with plastic utensils, drink from a separate water fountain, and use a reserved bathroom. By the time he arrived back at Western Middle School, half the school's students had been withdrawn by their parents. Before the end of the day, White was yanked back out by a court order requested by a group called Concerned Citizens and Parents of Children Attending Western School Corporation. They sued the Whites, their doctor, and the school for "endangering" three students. They tried to get Jeane White declared an unfit mother and have Ryan removed from her home.

When their case was finally heard, it took the judge less than a minute to throw out the case. Ryan returned to the school the same day. Shortly after Valentine's Day 1987, his locker was vandalized, with "Queer" and "Faggot" written on his school books. After a bullet was shot through the front window of their home while the family was at church, the family decided they'd had enough of Kokomo. With a loan from Elton John, the Whites moved to a new home in Cicero.

While some in Kokomo still try to explain the actions of so many in their community as "not enough information, too early in the epidemic," the reception the Whites received in Cicero, just 30 miles down the road, demonstrated that many people were capable of acting in a compassionate, rational manner.

White's Former Home, 3506 S. Webster St., Kokomo, IN 46902

Private phone

Hours: Private property; view from street

Cost: Free

Directions: Three blocks west of Rte. 31 on Southway Blvd., north four blocks on Webster St.

Western Middle School, 2600 S. County Road 600W, Russiaville, IN 46979

(765) 883-5566

Hours: Always visible, view from street

Cost: Free

Directions: Just south of County Rd. 250S on County Rd. 600W; the Middle School is on the west side of the street.

Kokomo
World's First Automobile

Ask any American who built the world's first successful commercial automobile and you're likely to get "Henry Ford" as an answer. But "Elwood Haynes"? Only in Kokomo.

When Haynes putted for six miles along Pumpkinvine Pike on July 4, 1894, he ushered in the age of the automobile. Town leaders had so little faith in the contraption they asked him to drive it outside the city limits, heading away from town. They thought it would scare horses, explode, or both. The experimental vehicle averaged 7 MPH, but it was a good start.

The car had been built by Edgar and Elmer Apperson under Elwood's direction. The trio formed a company in 1898 called the Haynes-Apperson Automobile Company, but split up and formed their own companies in 1902.

Haynes accomplishments were not limited to the automobile. In 1906 he invented stellite, a versatile metal alloy, and in 1912 he created stainless steel. You'll learn this and many other facts at the Elwood Haynes Museum, located in his former home, where he lived from 1915 to 1925. You won't see his original vehicle, however, because Haynes donated it to the Smithsonian in 1910. If you'd like to see other classic cars, visit Kokomo's Automotive Heritage Museum [1500 N. Reed Rd., (765) 454-9999] on the east side of town.

Elwood Haynes Museum, 1915 S. Webster St., Kokomo, IN 46902

(765) 456-7500

Hours: Tuesday–Saturday 1–4 P.M., Sunday 1–5 P.M.

Cost: Free

members.iquest.net/~deglen/haynes.html

Directions: On the east side of Highland Park, four blocks south of Defenbaugh St., two
   blocks west of Washington St.

**Haynes Monument, Pumpkinvine Pike (East Boulevard) & S. Goyer Rd. (Rte. 150E),
   Kokomo, IN 46902**

(800) 837-0971

Hours: Always visible

Cost: Free

Directions: East on East Blvd. off Rte. 31, just past the railroad crossing at Goyer Rd.

HARTFORD CITY
DeWayne Donathan and his wife came across two aliens in silver jump-suits dancing on Route 126 near Hartford City on October 22, 1973. Another driver, Gary Flatter, saw them two hours later, boogying in a plowed field. They wore some type of gas masks and were scared off by his truck's headlights.

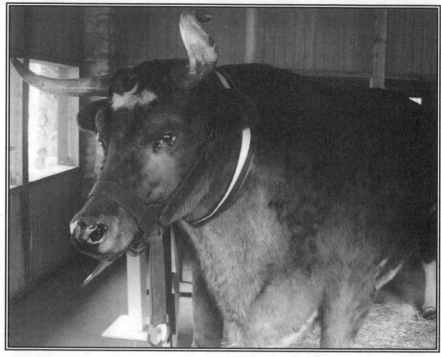

A lot of bull.

World's Largest Steer and World's Largest Sycamore Stump

It is special enough to be able to visit the stuffed remains of the World's Largest Steer, but to discover that it sits next to the World's Largest Sycamore Stump? It's too good to be true! No, you're not in Road Trip Heaven, you're in Kokomo.

Old Ben was a lot of bull . . . er . . . steer. He weighed 135 pounds when he was born in 1902 on the Murphy farm in Miami County. At a year and a half he was up to 1,800 pounds, and by the time he was four years old, over 4,000. Old Ben became a local celebrity and toured the local fairs. Tragedy struck in February 1910 when the eight-year-old bovine slipped on a patch of ice and broke his leg. At the time he weighed 4,720 pounds, stood 6 feet, 4 inches tall, and was more than 16 feet from nose to tail. Old Ben had to be destroyed, but when a local butcher suggested selling his meat to the local community, the locals responded with an emphatic "NO!" Instead, Old Ben was shipped off to a meat packer in Indy. His hide was stuffed and returned to the farm. It was eventually donated to the city and placed in the windowed shed where you can find him today.

The tale of the World's Largest Sycamore Stump is every bit as dramatic as that of Old Ben. This tree grew for 800-something years along the banks of Wildcat Creek on Tilghman Harrell's farm, two miles north of New London, before being felled by a violent windstorm. The hollowed-out trunk was moved to town in 1916 and used for some time as a phone booth. Today, the stump, with a 57-foot circumference, is protected from the public in a special shed in Highland Park.

Highland Park, 1402 W. Defenbaugh, Kokomo, IN 46902

(765) 456-7275

Hours: Daily 8 A.M.–10 P.M.

Cost: Free

members.iquest.net/~deglen/oldben.html

Directions: Five blocks south of Markland Ave., at the north end of the park.

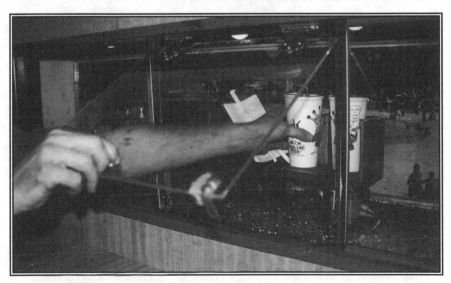

Dinner is served!

Lafayette
Pizza King

If you drive around Indiana enough, you'll think there's a Pizza King in every town with a stoplight. This Hoosier franchise started on the south side of Lafayette at a venue that still stands, and it is perhaps the strangest restaurant in the state.

The carpeted booths seem more like office cubicles than restaurant furniture; their backs are so high you won't see any other patrons except those directly across the aisle. This is good, because each booth is outfitted with its own coin-operated television. If your date's a drag, just pop a quarter into the control box in the wall, and you'll get 15 minutes of video entertainment. Magic Fingers for your brain.

To place an order, pick up the tableside phone—no waitstaff here! Your drinks will arrive on a toy train that runs along the booths, protected by a clear plastic window, and decorated with scenes from Lafayette area attractions. Don't worry that another customer can slip you a Mickey; only the trap door at the destination booth can be opened when the train is in operation.

And the pizza? Well . . . the trains and TV make up for a lot. . . .

Jefferson Square, 9th St. & Teal Rd., Lafayette, IN 47905

(765) 474-3414

Hours: Sunday–Thursday 11 A.M.–11 P.M., Friday–Saturday 11 A.M.–1 A.M.

Cost: Meals $5–$10

Directions: Across from the Tippecanoe Fairgrounds, east of 9th St.

LAFAYETTE
Lafayette has sometimes been derided by local towns as "Laugh-at" or "Lay-flat."

Clown **Emmett Kelly**, creator of Wearie Willie, is buried in Lafayette's Rest Haven Memorial Park Cemetery (1200 N. Sagamore Parkway).

Guns 'N' Roses singer **Axl Rose** was born William Baily in Lafayette on February 6, 1962.

Bubble wash, hot wax, or shrunken head?
Courtesy of the Rainforest Car Wash

Rainforest Car Wash

No road trip through central Indiana would be complete without a stop by the Rainforest Car Wash. "What?" you ask, "A jungle in the Midwest?" Sure enough, and, though it is adjacent to a shopping mall, it is in no way related to a certain unnamed, overpriced, mall-based restaurant chain with the same theme.

When you pull up, a giant tiki head examines your vehicle with its mechanical eyes. Roll down your window to hear the beating drums. Attendants dressed in safari clothes give you a variety of options. Every cleaning option here has a name: the Froggy Pre-Wash, the Monkey Soapy Wash, the Snakey Foamy Brush, the Crocodile Wax, the Rhino Tire Clean, the Elephant High-Pressure Wash, and the Macaw Spot-Free Rinse. Once you pay, your guide directs you to the tree-filled wash tunnel and informs you to roll up your window—it seems that wild animals are loose!

Sure enough, snakes and monkeys hang from the sprayers, toucans perch atop spinning scrubbers, and elephants poke their heads out from between the machines. Sadly, these jungle creatures are only robots. The only reason to keep the windows up is to keep the soap out of your eyes. Lion Country Safari it ain't—but it's a wonderful wash.

2507 Maple Point Dr., Lafayette, IN 47905

(765) 446-9438

Hours: Monday–Saturday 8 A.M.–8 P.M., Sunday 11 A.M.–6 P.M.

Cost: Basic $5.95, Gorilla Wash $7.95–$9.95, Crocodile Wash $11.95

Directions: Off Rte. 38, east of Rte. 52, on the southeast side of the Tippecanoe Mall.

LAFAYETTE
The first U.S. air mail took off in a balloon from Lafayette on August 17, 1859, headed for New York. The *Jupiter*, piloted by John Wise, only got as far as Crawfordsville. The letters traveled the rest of the way by train.

LAUREL
A double UFO was spotted near Laurel on October 11, 1973, by five men. The craft was scared off when one of the men blew the horn on his truck.

LEBANON
William "Captain Kirk" **Shatner** married his fourth wife, Elizabeth Martin, in Lebanon on February 13, 2001.

LIBERTY
Ambrose Burnside, Union Civil War general and "inventor" of side-burns, was born in Liberty on May 23, 1824 (1.6 miles east of the courthouse on Rte. 27).

Marion
James Dean's Birthplace

On February 8, 1931, Winton and Mildred Dean became the proud parents of a boy they named James Byron Dean. They lived in the Green Gables apartments until young Jimmy was three, and his father came up with a harebrained scheme to raise bullfrogs for profit in nearby Fairmount. The trio moved into a house at Washington and Vine Streets, but, as you might expect with frog farms, the orders didn't come rolling in. Soon, the family left for California so his dad could accept a position at a Los Angeles V.A. hospital.

As big a star as James Dean was, very little marks his birthplace. The Green Gables were torn down long ago and the land used for a tire store parking lot. A bronze star is embedded in the sidewalk to mark the historic site, along with a small plaque near a bus stop bench.

Marion Tire, 302 E. 4th St., Marion, IN 46953

(765) 664-6460

Hours: Always visible

Cost: Free

Directions: Two blocks east of the courthouse on E. 4th (Rte. 18), on the southwest
corner of E. 4th and S. McClure Sts.

Milan
The Real Hoosiers

There are few things in Indiana more important than basketball. Mom and her apple pie can just wait in the bleachers when the spring tournament, "Hoosier Hysteria," rolls around. Because Indiana does not rank its high schools by size, theoretically every school's team has a shot at the state title. One team, known as the "Milan Miracle," pulled off just such an upset in 1954.

In 1953, the Milan team made it to the state semifinals, so it was not like this was a complete fluke. They had talent, but it was remarkable that they could field a team of 12 out of only 75 boys in the student body. To make a verrrry long story short, the Milan David slew the Muncie Central Goliath 32–30 with a last-second, 18-foot jump shot by Bobby Plump. If you want the full story, ask anyone around Milan and reserve several hours in your day.

The 1987 movie *Hoosiers*, with Gene Hackman and Dennis Hopper, is loosely based on Milan's championship season. The fictitious town is named Hickory and the exterior locations were shot in New Richmond.

The old Milan High School has been traded in for a new model, though they brought along part of the original gym floor, the scoreboard, and the championship trophy. More Milan Miracle mementos are on display at an antique store downtown.

Old Milan High School, Carr St. & Lakeside Dr., Milan, IN 47031
No phone
Hours: Never visible; torn down
Cost: Free
Directions: East one block on Carr St. from Rte. 101, turn north on Lakeside Dr.

Milan Station Antiques & Collectibles, 113 Carr St., PO Box 296, Milan, IN 47031
(812) 654-2772
E-mail: rvmckitt@seidata.com
Hours: Thursday–Saturday 10 A.M.–4 P.M., Sunday noon–4 P.M.
Cost: Free
Directions: Two blocks east of Rte. 101 on Carr St., one block south of the railroad
   tracks.

Milan High School (Today), 609 Warpath Dr., Milan, IN 47031
(812) 654-3096
Hours: Call for an appointment
Cost: Free
Directions: South of Rte. 350 on Rte. 101.

MUNCIE

Many of the opening scenes of *Close Encounters of the Third Kind* were set in Muncie, though they were not filmed there.

Fishing tackle is not allowed in Muncie cemeteries.

So you're the guy who chopped down all the trees!

Muncie
Barfly Cortez and the Lumberjack

If you're a business owner who wants to attract attention for your establishment, there are several ways to go about it. Advertising. Coupons. Jumbo statues of disproportionate humans standing out by the road.

Two watering holes in Muncie have used the third strategy. The Oasis Bar & Grill, on the south side, has a chainsaw-carved totem of basketballer Barfly Cortez. Never heard of him? Well, the 20-foot figure looks a lot like

Larry Bird, with flat white skin and 33 on his jersey. His alias seems to have fooled lawyers concerned with licensing issues.

Oasis Bar & Grill, 1811 S. Burlington Dr., Muncie, IN 47302

(765) 282-8326

Hours: Always visible

Cost: Free

Directions: At the corner of E. Memorial Dr. and Burlington Dr.

The 30-foot lumberjack outside the Timbers Lounge doesn't seem to have a famous counterpart, though he does look a lot like a Mafia turncoat with a fake beard and mustache. He's made of fiberglass and carries a large ax, so wisecracks about the facial hair are best kept to yourself.

Timbers Lounge, 2770 W. Kilgore Ave., Muncie, IN 47307

(765) 286-5323

Hours: Always visible

Cost: Free

Directions: At the corner of Tillotson Ave. and Kilgore Ave. (Rte. 52).

David Letterman, C Student

When David Letterman attended Ball State during the 1960s, his ironic sensibility had yet to pay off, or at least pay off in a positive way. His first broadcasting gig came as a student DJ on the campus classical station, WBST, a 10-watt station. One evening he introduced Debussy's *Clair de lune* by asking aloud, "You know the de Lune sisters? There was Claire, there was Mabel . . ." Letterman was promptly canned.

His next "job" was at WAGO, a pirate station run from a men's dorm, followed by a position at local outlet WERK. He worked harder at his broadcasting career than his broadcasting major, graduating with a C average. If Letterman was embarrassed about his academic performance, all that went out the window in 1985 when he established the Letterman Scholarship for telecommunications students with C averages—brainiacs need not apply! He also paid to update the Communication Department's television and radio studios, complete with a plaque that reads, "Dedicated to all the C students before and after me."

Ball Communications Building, McKinley Ave. & Petty Rd., Muncie, IN 47306

(765) 285-1480

Hours: Daily 9 A.M.–5 P.M.

Cost: Free

www.tcom.bsu.edu/program3.htm

Directions: Two blocks north of Riverside Ave. on McKinley Ave.

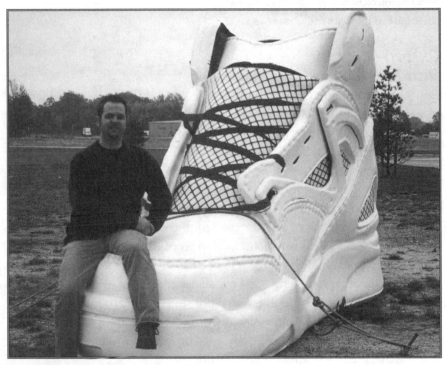

You know what they say about big shoes . . . Photo by James Frost

New Castle
Big Sneaker

Steve Alford has an impressive basketball resume: Indiana's "Mr. Basketball" in 1983, gold medal winner at the 1984 Olympics, four-year starter at Indiana University under Bobby Knight, second-round draft pick for the Dallas Mavericks, traded two years later to the Golden State Warriors, and current head coach at the University of Iowa. And though that all sounds soooooo impressive, you might think differently after stopping by the guy's hotel in his home town of New Castle. Why? The guy couldn't help but win, he's HUGE! Just look at his Volkswagen-sized sneaker—how could any opponent go up against *that*?

Steve Alford All-American Inn, 21 E. Executive Dr., New Castle, IN 47362

(765) 593-1212

Hours: Always visible

Cost: Free; Rooms $49–$75

www.ez-look.com/stevealfordinn/index.html

Directions: At the south end of town on Rte. 3.

Oxford
Dan Patch, Gone

Dan Messner thought he had a bum colt. Foaled at Messner's Oxford farm to sire Joe Patchen and dam Zelica in December 1896, Dan Patch had bowed legs, the curse of a harness racer. Messner tried to trade Dan Patch to a local horse trainer named John Wattles, but Wattles turned him down. Dan Patch raced in county fairs, but his career was undistinguished.

Messner finally sold the horse to M. E. Sturgis of New York in 1902, who in turn sold him to Marion W. Savage of Minneapolis. In greener pastures, Dan Patch went on to set a world record for the mile, 1:55. This record time stood for 32 years, and is still painted on the roof of the barn where the horse was born in Oxford.

Dan Patch never lost a race and came in second only twice during heats. The secret of his success was discovered only after his death in 1916; his heart was twice the size of a normal horse's heart, weighing a whopping 9 pounds, 2 ounces. Owner Marion Savage, whose heart was not as strong as Dan Patch's, died a day after his famous horse.

Rtes. 352 & 55, Oxford, IN 47971

No phone

Hours: Always visible

Cost: Free

Directions: Northeast of the intersection of Rtes. 352 & 55.

NEW CASTLE

The American Beauty Rose was developed in New Castle in 1901 by Myer and Herbert Heller.

Uncle Bill . . .ooooh, noooooooooooo!

Richmond
Keeping Up with the Joneses

Jim Jones attended Richmond High after his parents separated during his junior year. To make a little cash, Jim took a job as an orderly at Reid Memorial Hospital. There he met Marceline Baldwin, his future wife.

Baldwin was a nurse at Reid Memorial, and was inexplicably attracted to the high schooler.

Jim's childhood friend, Don Foreman, was also an orderly at Reid. Jones would terrorize him by turning out the lights when Foreman swept the tunnel connecting the hospital to the nurses' quarters, or by leaving realistic anatomical models for him to find where he least expected it.

Reid Memorial, 1401 Chester Blvd., Richmond, IN 47374

(765) 983-3000

Hours: Always visible

Cost: Free

Directions: On the north side of town on Rte. 27 (Chester Blvd.).

Jim wasn't the only wacky Jones in Richmond. His Uncle Bill committed suicide by jumping off the G Street Bridge.

G St. Bridge, Richmond, IN 47374

No phone

Hours: Always visible

Cost: Free

Directions: Take S. G St. west four blocks from Rte. 27, at S. 5th St.

Terre Haute
Birthplace of the Curvaceous Coke Bottle

For many years, Coca-Cola was sold in a standard glass bottle. Ho hum. Then, in 1913, the company launched a manufacturers' competition to devise a unique bottle. A fellow named T. Clyde Edwards, working for Terre Haute's Root Glass Works, saw a drawing of a bulging, ribbed cocoa bean pod and modeled what later became known as the "hobble skirt" or "Mae West" bottle after it. Edwards was assisted by Alexander Samuelson in devising a manufacturing process, and in 1916, Coke launched its new look. Samuelson and Root owned the patent until 1937.

The original hobble skirt was much fatter in the middle than today's bottle, as you can see at the Vigo County Museum. They have one of the Root Glass Works's original molds, a bottle formed inside it, and display cases crammed with Coke memorabilia.

Thornton Oil Corp/80 (former site of Root Glass Works), 2330 S. 3rd St., Terre Haute,
  IN 47802

(812) 234-3102

Hours: Always visible

Cost: Free

Directions: On the northeast corner of S. 3rd St. (Rte. 41/150) and Voorhees St.

Vigo County Museum, 1411 S. 6th St., Terre Haute, IN 47802

(812) 235-9717

E-mail: vchs@iquest.net

Hours: Tuesday–Sunday 1–4 P.M.

Cost: Free

web.indstate.edu/community/vchs/

Directions: At the corner of Washington Ave. and S. 6th St.

Chuck, Tim, and the Unabomber

The U.S. Penitentiary in Terre Haute used to deal with a lower caliber of federal criminal. The prison was home to Chuck Berry for two years, from 1962 to 1964, for violating the Mann Act. The rocker had been found guilty of taking a 14-year-old girl across state lines for "immoral purposes."

When the federal government moved its Death House operations here in the 1990s, it attracted some real violent folk. It was here, on June 11, 2001, that Timothy McVeigh was executed for the mass murder of 168 citizens in Oklahoma City. It is also where the Unabomber, Theodore Kaczynski, is spending the rest of his life.

U.S. Penitentiary, Rte. 63 & 45th Dr., Terre Haute, IN 47802

(812) 238-1531

Hours: Always visible

Cost: Free

www.bop.gov

Directions: At the intersection of Prairieton Rd. (Rte. 63) and Bureau Dr. on the southwest side of town, along the river.

TERRE HAUTE

The Socialist Party's perennial presidential candidate, labor leader **Eugene Debs**, was born at 457 N. 4th Street in Terre Haute on November 5, 1855. Though his birthplace has been torn down, his adult home still stands and is a museum open for tours (451 N. 8th St.).

It's not just the donuts that are square.
Photo by Jim Frost

Square Donuts

First the Coke bottle, and now this? What will those crafty Terre Hauteans come up with next? The concept is brilliant in its simplicity. By making a donut square, you can do one of two things: either fit more donuts onto the same sized tray, or fit larger donuts on the same size tray. Either way you maximize donut capacity!

Square donut technology is still in its infancy, for although the outer edges of these delightful pastries are square, their holes are still round. No doubt somebody is trying to crack that challenge in some bakery's backroom laboratory.

Even if the donuts weren't square, they'd be worth a stop—not quite Krispy Kremes, but as close as you'll get around here. They've got three locations in town, one on the south side, one on the north side, and one downtown.

Square Donuts, 1842 S. 3rd St., Terre Haute, IN 47802

(812) 232-6463

Hours: Monday–Saturday 6 A.M.–6 P.M.

Cost: $3.95/dozen

Directions: Four blocks north of Voorhees St. on S. 3rd St. (Rte. 41/150).

Square Donuts, 9th & Wabash, Terre Haute, IN 47807

No phone

Hours: Monday–Saturday 6–11 A.M.

Cost: $3.95/dozen

Directions: Six blocks east of 3rd St. (Rte. 41) on Wabash (Rte. 40).

Square Donuts, N. 25th St. & Fort Harrison Rd., Terre Haute, IN 47804

No phone

Hours: Monday–Saturday 6–11 A.M.

Cost: $3.95/dozen

Directions: Five blocks east of Lafayette Ave. on Ft. Harrison Rd.

Stiffy Green, the Stiff Dog

The story has been passed between generations of Terre Hauteans. When he was alive, Stiffy Green followed John Heinl everywhere, and when Heinl died in 1920, the loyal bulldog was so distraught he sat outside Heinl's tomb to guard his dead master. Stiffy wouldn't eat, and before long was soon found dead beside the mausoleum. Somebody got the bright idea to stuff the faithful dog and place him inside the tomb to guard the vault for eternity.

Local teens would head out to the cemetery to peer through the bars where, according to legend, Stiffy would stare back with glowing green eyes or wag his tail. Other visitors have claimed to have spotted the ghosts of Heinl, smoking a pipe, and Stiffy strolling through the graveyard at night, together again.

Too bad it's all a fabrication. In reality, Stiffy is very stiff—he's made of concrete! The dog once stood outside the Heinl home in town, and later inside the family crypt. After years of vandalism, Stiffy was removed in 1985 and donated to the local historical society, where you can find him today inside a re-created tomb. And Heinl's tomb in Highland Lawn? Empty . . . except for the Heinls.

Highland Lawn Cemetery, 4520 Wabash Ave., Terre Haute, IN 47808

(812) 877-2531

Hours: Daily 9 A.M.–5 P.M.

Cost: Free

Directions: Head east on Wabash Ave. (Rte. 40) from downtown, on the left just past the railroad overpass.

Vigo County Museum, 1411 S. 6th St., Terre Haute, IN 47802

(812) 235-9717

E-mail: vchs@iquest.net

Hours: Tuesday–Sunday 1–4 P.M.

Cost: Free

web.indstate.edu/community/vchs/

Directions: At the corner of Washington Ave. and S. 6th St.

FUNKY GRAVES IN HIGHLAND LAWN

So, Stiffy's no longer at Highland Lawn. No matter—there are still plenty of interesting monuments to see at this well-maintained graveyard.

First, check out the mausoleum of **Martin Sheets**. It has a chandelier and a telephone inside. Sheets was afraid he would be buried alive, so he had the phone installed to link him to the caretaker's office. Local legend says he also put whisky bottles in the pillars of the tomb, no doubt for something to drink until the caretaker arrived. Still wilder claims say flowers appear inside the crypt, even when nobody has brought them.

The plot of **John Robert Craig** resembles a bed. The traveling salesman died of a heart attack while having sex with a woman other than his wife in an Indianapolis hotel room on New Year's Eve, 1931. Craig's wife commissioned his headstone and coldly observed, "He made his bed. Now he'll lie in it."

Just inside the main gate is a globe-shaped marker marking the grave of **Frank Wiedemann**, developer of the X-ray machine. Wiedemann used the profits from his invention to become a world traveler, hence the tombstone.

Finally, Socialist and labor leader **Eugene Debs** is interred somewhere in his family's plot, but for security reasons, the exact location is a secret.

World's First Pay Toilets

Time to review a few Terre Haute inventions. Curvaceous Coke bottles? Great! Square donuts? Delicious! Pay toilets? Talk about getting you coming and going . . .

Back when there were more railroads running through town, Union Station sat at the intersection of north–south and east–west lines near downtown. The modern station installed what was, apparently, a newfangled luxury at the time: public toilets. The trouble was, so many of the locals were stopping by for a visit that the paying customers were waiting for a seat. So in 1910 the stationmaster started charging 5¢ a visit—unless you were a ticket-carrying passenger—and the pay toilet was born.

Union Station, 10th & Wabash Sts., Terre Haute, IN 47807

No phone

Hours: Station torn down

Cost: 5¢

Directions: Campus Lot J on Wabash between 9½ and 10th Sts.

Thorntown
Crown of Thorntown

The idea came to Reverend Alan Moody in a dream: build a giant, crown-shaped garden, fill it with religious symbolism, and the faithful will flock to Thorntown to praise God's glory! The exterior wall went up, each of its six peaks topped with a glowing orb. Inside the walls, a wayside chapel was erected, baptismal pools were dug, and shrubbery was placed along the narrow pathways.

But unlike in *Field of Dreams*, after Moody built it, the folks did not come. Today, the Garden of Memories is becoming just that. With its aqua, cement-lined pools drained and weeds sprouting up everywhere, it looks more like an abandoned putt-putt course than royal headwear for the Most High. Still, the chapel is open if you'd like to say a prayer for this folly of the faithful.

Garden of Memories, Walnut Grove Chapel of Praise, 8995 Rte. 52, Thorntown, IN 46035

(765) 436-7029

Hours: Always open; Services, Sunday 10:30 A.M., Wednesday 7 P.M.

Cost: Free

Directions: North of town five miles on Rte. 52, near Brush Creek.

Hoosiers to the left, Buckeyes to the right.

West College Corner and Union City
Towns Torn in Half

In a world filled with ethnic and regional strife, we should all look to two Indiana/Ohio communities as examples of harmony and togetherness. Take West College Corner, Indiana, and College Corner, Ohio. The state border runs through the middle of these towns, which requires that they have different mayors, fire departments, water systems, and taxes—but they have only one post office, united under ZIP codes 47003 (IN) and 45003 (OH). During daylight savings time the towns sit in different time zones, so you can leave work in College Corner and arrive home in West College Corner before you punched out. On the downside, you can leave your home in Indiana for a five-minute commute to Ohio and pull into your job an hour late. Still, somehow it all works out.

Even more amazing is the town of Union City, where a local elementary straddles the border at the north end of State Line Street. Over the school's west entrance is a sign saying "Indiana," and over the east entrance is a sign that says "Ohio."

Union School, Stateline & Ramsey Sts., Union City, IN 45390

Private phone

Hours: Always visible

Cost: Free

Directions: Head north on Stateline St., five blocks north of where the railroad tracks cross Rte. 27.

Michael Craig was here . . .

Windfall
Michael Craig Sculpture Garden

It peeks at you over the top of a main street storefront like a modern-day Kilroy, the top of a head whose big blue eyes stare down on a crumbling town. Is it watching for vandals in the sculpture garden below? The only person who knows for sure is the guy who made him, Michael Craig. This creative welder has built a small-scale "garden" of 10-foot metal flowers and creatures on a vacant lot in the heart of Windfall. Some of his pieces have seen better days, so you'd better see them while you still have the chance.

Sherman St. & Rte. 213, Windfall, IN 46076

(765) 945-8226

Hours: Always visible

Cost: Free

Directions: On the northeast corner of Rte. 213 and County Rd. 400N (Sherman St.).

Big Jack eats Winnebagos for breakfast.

Yorktown
Big Jack

Big Jack! He's got a big head, and a bigger appetite! Heck, I've seen him eat a whole Winnebago—driver, too—with one gulp. You might think a 30-foot, camper-eating monster would be the wrong mascot of an RV dealership, but that was what the elves thought about the Abominable Snowman in *Rudolph, the Red-Nosed Reindeer*, and look at how that worked out.

So here stands Big Jack, glaring out at the traffic on I-69, a vehicle resting in his open palm. He gladly guards the brand-new models, as long as they give him the trade-ins for dinner.

Jack Smith & Son RV Center, 3400 N. Lee Pit Rd., Yorktown, IN 47396

(800) 878-2130

Hours: Always visible

Cost: Free

www.jacksmithrv.com

Directions: Exit 41 (Rte. 332) from I-69, just west of the interstate.

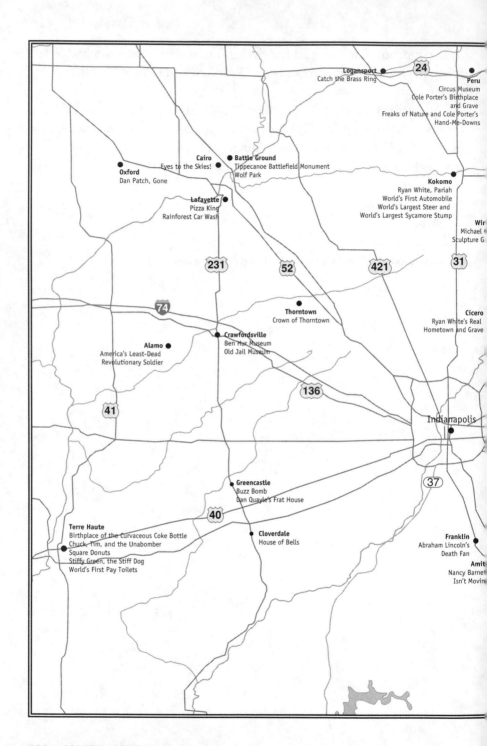

Logansport
Catch the Brass Ring

24

Peru
Circus Museum
Cole Porter's Birthplace
and Grave
Freaks of Nature and Cole Porter's
Hand-Me-Downs

Cairo
Eyes to the Skies!

Battle Ground
Tippecanoe Battlefield Monument
Wolf Park

Oxford
Dan Patch, Gone

Kokomo
Ryan White, Pariah
World's First Automobile
World's Largest Steer and
World's Largest Sycamore Stump

Lafayette
Pizza King
Rainforest Car Wash

Wir
Michael
Sculpture G

231   52   421   31

Thorntown
Crown of Thorntown

Cicero
Ryan White's Real
Hometown and Grave

74

Alamo
America's Least-Dead
Revolutionary Soldier

Crawfordsville
Ben Hur Museum
Old Jail Museum

136

41

Indianapolis

Greencastle
Buzz Bomb
Dan Quayle's Frat House

37

40

Terre Haute
Birthplace of the Curvaceous Coke Bottle
Chuck, Tim, and the Unabomber
Square Donuts
Stiffy Green, the Stiff Dog
World's First Pay Toilets

Cloverdale
House of Bells

Franklin
Abraham Lincoln's
Death Fan

Amit
Nancy Barne
Isn't Movin

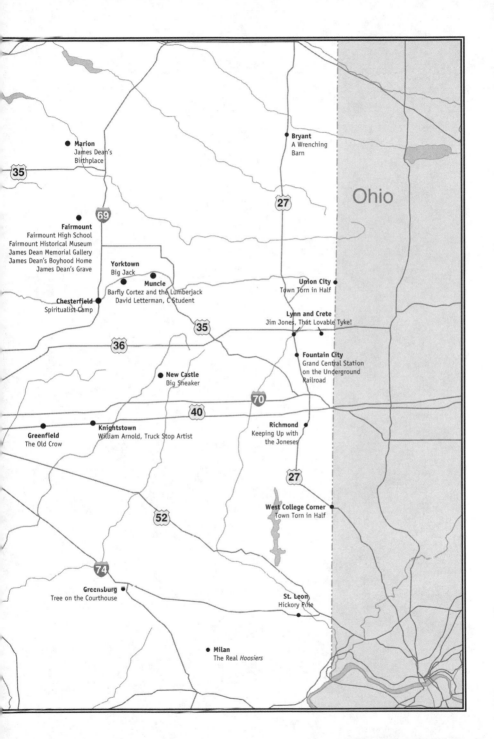

Marion
James Dean's
Birthplace

Bryant
A Wrenching
Barn

35

27

Ohio

69

Fairmount
Fairmount High School
Fairmount Historical Museum
James Dean Memorial Gallery
James Dean's Boyhood Home
James Dean's Grave

Yorktown
Big Jack

Muncie
Barfly Cortez and the Lumberjack
David Letterman, C Student

Union City
Town Torn in Half

Chesterfield
Spiritualist Camp

Lynn and Crete
Jim Jones, That Lovable Tyke!

35

36

Fountain City
Grand Central Station
on the Underground
Railroad

New Castle
Big Sneaker

40

70

Greenfield
The Old Crow

Knightstown
William Arnold, Truck Stop Artist

Richmond
Keeping Up with
the Joneses

27

52

West College Corner
Town Torn in Half

74

Greensburg
Tree on the Courthouse

St. Leon
Hickory Pole

Milan
The Real *Hoosiers*

3

SOUTHERN INDIANA

Something strange happens when you reach southern Indiana. As the state's cornfields turn upward into gentle hills, the region takes on a Kentucky sensibility. The land of Wonder Bread and Dan Quayle turns to creepy limestone monuments and the Bluegrass Hall of Fame. They've got museums to old steamboats and statues of Joe Palooka, trees draped in discarded shoes, haunted libraries, and the one-of-a-kind Museum of All Sorts of Stuff.

And southern Indiana has more than just hillbilly attractions; they've got international places to visit that would take years to see in their original locations. On a three-day weekend you can explore a town named after Santa Claus, a Tibetan Culture Center, a crumbling Egyptian pyramid, and the footprints of the angel Gabriel—yet never leave the state. So forget skiing to the North Pole, trekking through the Himalayas, jetting to the Middle East, or flying off to heaven. Southern Indiana has it all, and more!

Bean Blossom
Bill Monroe Country Star Museum & Campground

Bill Monroe has been dubbed the Father of Bluegrass (not to be confused with Jimmy Martin, the *King* of Bluegrass), and indeed, few folks have done more to preserve this uniquely American musical form. Monroe and his family have hosted the Bean Blossom Bluegrass Festival every spring since the mid 1960s. Performers have included some of the biggest names in country music, and if you step into the museum you can see the outfits they wore: Dolly Parton, Johnny Cash, Loretta Lynn, George Jones, Stringbean, and more. Never heard of Stringbean? You won't forget his costume. If you think hip-hop artists invented the pants-down-around-your-knees style, think again!

Back behind the museum is Uncle Pen's Cabin, Monroe's tribute to his Uncle Pendleton Vandiver. Uncle Pen taught Monroe to pick, and he has ended up in many of the performer's best-known songs. You're invited to meet Uncle Pen, but he turns out to be a stuffed mannequin, which is a little creepy. If you'd like to set a spell, stay at the adjacent campground or rent a log cabin. The museum currently hosts four annual music festivals, so there are plenty of opportunities to listen to banjo pickin' all night long.

5163 State Road 135N, Bean Blossom, IN 46160

(800) 414-4677 or (812) 988-6422

E-mail: beanblossombg@hotmail.com

Hours: May–November, Monday–Saturday 9 A.M.–5 P.M., Sunday 1–5 P.M.;

    December–April, Monday–Saturday 10 A.M.–4 P.M.

Cost: Adults $4, Seniors $3, Kids (12 and under) free

www.beanblossom.com

Directions: Five mile north of Nashville on Rte. 135, just north of the Rte. 45
    intersection.

BREWERSVILLE

Gigantic skeletons, one 9'8" tall and wearing a mica necklace, were excavated from a burial mound near Brewersville (near where Rte. 3 crosses the Sand River) in 1879. The bones were kept on the Robinson farm until a flood swept them away in 1937.

Something's a Foote.

Bedford
Foote's Tomb and the Bedford Cemetery

Bedford has long been the focal point of limestone quarrying operations in southern Indiana. With so many expert stonecarvers around, you'd expect the monuments in the local cemeteries to be out of this world. Sadly, the graveyards here look much like everywhere else . . . with a few notable exceptions.

The best tomb in town isn't in a cemetery at all, but carved into a stone outcropping by "Mr. Toburn" in 1840 for a town leader, Dr. Winthrop Foote. The doctor wanted a spot to inter his brother, Ziba, who drowned in 1806. When Toburn was done, Ziba was moved into a room in the hollowed-out boulder. Winthrop died in 1856 and was placed there, too, though details of the burial were lost. That's why locals were so shocked when vandals broke into the vault in 1957. Apparently, Winthrop had himself placed in a mummylike coffin with gun and ammo at his feet, along with his doctor's bag. Ziba, as expected, was in another room, but a third chamber contained a horse's corpse. The tomb was resealed as it was discovered, and remains closed to this day.

Bedford's Green Hill Cemetery contains some unique markers. One shows a limestone re-creation of young, unlucky stonemason Louis Baker's sloppy workbench on the day he died in 1917. Another monument, this one for Tom Barton, is a full-sized replica of the man and his set of stone golf clubs, as if Barton has a tee time in Bedrock. World War I soldier Michael Wallner is re-created in his doughboy's uniform; and a dead girl's straw hat and shoes rest, re-created in stone, beneath a carved tree over her head.

Foote's Tomb, E. 16th & D Sts., Bedford, IN 47421

No phone

Hours: Always visible

Cost: Free

Directions: Follow the stone markers down the hill 250 feet, bearing left, from E. 16th St. (Rte. 50) at D St., behind the used car lot.

Green Hill Cemetery, 1202 18th St., Bedford, IN 47421

(812) 275-5110

Daily 9 A.M.–5 P.M.

Cost: Free

Directions: At L St., one block east and two blocks south of the Rte. 50/450 intersection. Cemetery maps available from the Lawrence County Tourism Bureau: (800) 798-0769.

Bloomington
Bobby Knight Meets Zero Tolerance

There is no better way to launch a no-holds-barred debate in Indiana than to ask a group of people their thoughts on Bobby Knight. For 29 years he coached the IU basketball squad and was no stranger to media controversy or the Final Four. To hear people describe him, there are two Coach Knights.

On one hand, there's Bobby Knight the B-Ball Prophet. Three NCAA national championships. Eleven Big Ten championships. A remarkably honest recruiting record. Outstanding player graduation rates. All true.

On the other hand, there's Bobby Knight the Out-of-Control Hot-head. Tossing a chair across the court at a 1985 game against Purdue. Wiping his rear end with toilet paper to illustrate to his players what he thought of their playing. Heaving a potted plant across the office of IU's athletic director. Bragging about mooning Puerto Rican officials as his U.S. team departed the San Juan airport after the 1979 Pan Am Games (though probably never did it). Kicking son Patrick during a game against Notre Dame in 1993.

When university president Dr. Myles Brand viewed videotape of Knight choking player Neil Reed at a 1997 practice, he instituted a Zero Tolerance policy for further bad behavior. It was amazing Knight lasted 17 weeks. But on September 7, 2000, Knight was headed to his office in Assembly Hall when freshman Kent Harvey dared to say, "Hey, what's up, Knight?" Bobby grabbed Harvey's arm roughly and said, "Son, my name is not Knight to you. It's Coach Knight or Mr. Knight!" Others claimed he added, "Show me some fucking respect. I'm older than you!" Three days later Knight was fired, and Harvey started getting death threats.

Assembly Hall, IU Campus, 1001 E. 17th St., Bloomington, IN 47408

(800) 447-GO-IU (447-4648)

Hours: Always visible

Cost: Free

www.indiana.edu/~athlweb/graphic/facil/assembly.html

The Dark Side of Bobby Knight Web site: www.members.aol.com/rmkgeneral

Directions: Just south of the Rte. 46 Bypass, at 17th St. & Fee Lane.

BLOOMINGTON

A triangular UFO was spotted on Rte. 45 between Bloomington and New Unionville on January 4, 2001.

David Lee Roth was born in Bloomington on October 10, 1955.

Hoagy Carmichael wrote his most famous tune, "Stardust," while sitting in Bloomington's Book Nook (114 S. University, since closed). He also wrote "As Time Goes By" here.

Don't jump! Photo by James Lane

Breaking Away

Ask anyone in Bloomington, "Where's the old quarry from *Breaking Away*?" and you'll always get the same response: "Oh, you can't go down there . . ." followed by a wink and an exact set of directions. The swimming hole plays a pivotal role in the 1980 movie, which follows the lives of four high school friends the summer after graduation. Too bad the thing's empty.

Argue if you will, *Hoosiers* fans, but *Breaking Away* is the best movie ever shot in Indiana, all filmed in and around Bloomington. Steve Tesich, a hometown boy, wrote the script that earned him an Oscar for Best Original Screenplay. Not bad for a "cutter."

If you can't find anyone to direct you out to the quarry—and why can't you?—there are other sites from the film to visit. Take a date to the IU Student Union (900 E. 7th St.), but don't throw a bowling ball through the trophy case. Have a heart to heart with your father outside the IU Library (10th St. & Jordan). Or grab a bike and ride through the Brown

County countryside, singing in Italian and chasing Cinzano trucks. It seems everyone else is. Sorry to say, the Little 500 Stadium on 10th Street was torn down not long after the movie was wrapped, though the race is still held each spring at a new facility.

Bloomington Visitor's Bureau, 2855 N. Walnut, Bloomington, IN 47404

(800) 800-0037

Hours: Monday–Friday 8:30 A.M.–5 P.M., Saturday 9 A.M.–4 P.M., Sunday 10 A.M.–3 P.M.

Cost: Free

www.visitbloomington.com

Little 500: iusf.bloomington.com/little5/little5.com

Directions: North of the Rte. 45/46 Bypass on Walnut (Business Rte. 37).

George Washington and the Prime Directive

Indiana University's Lilly Library, being both young and well endowed, has a rare book collection like no other. It has George Washington's acceptance letter for the presidency and the complete scripts of *Star Trek: The Next Generation*. You can find a Gutenberg Bible and Thomas Jefferson's copy of the Bill of Rights next to movie scripts for *Citizen Kane*, *Jaws*, *The Godfather*, and *Gone With the Wind*. They've got a copy of the first children's book, *The History of Little Goody Two Shoes* (John Newberry, 1768); as well as television scripts from *Hazel*, *The Mary Tyler Moore Show*, *I Love Lucy*, and the complete annotated scripts from *Laugh-In*. A recent donation from Peter Bogdanovich puts the Lilly in possession of *Paper Moon* and *What's Up Doc?* scripts.

For obvious reasons, the collection is not open for the general public to thumb through—if they did, there would be a lot of Trekkies violating the Prime Directive. But the Lilly Library does have rotating displays of some of their more interesting specimens.

Lilly Library of Rare Books and Manuscripts, Fine Arts Plaza, 1200 E. 7th St., Bloomington, IN 47405

(812) 855-2452

E-mail: liblilly@indiana.edu

Hours: Monday–Friday 9 A.M.–6 P.M. (5 P.M. summers), Saturday 9 A.M.–1 P.M.

Cost: Free

www.indiana.edu/~liblilly/text/lillyhome.html

Directions: Between E. University Rd. and N. Jordan Ave.

So tell me, how many times a week do you . . . well . . . you know. . .
Photo by James Lane

Kinsey Institute for Research in Sex, Gender, and Reproduction

When university entomologist Alfred Kinsey changed his field of study from the gall wasp to human sexuality in the 1940s, he probably never guessed the impact he would have on society. He founded the Institute for Sex Research in 1942, and in 1948 kicked open the door on this taboo subject with the landmark publication of *Sexual Behavior in the American Male*. He followed it with *Sexual Behavior of the American Female* in 1953. Many believe these two studies, by shining light on issues like female orgasms, homosexuality, and erotica, ushered in the Sexual Revolution.

While in Bloomington, Kinsey lived at 620 S. Fess St. (1921), 615 S. Park St. (1921– 1927), and 1320 E. First St. (1927–1956). He died on August 25, 1956, and was buried in Rose Hill Cemetery. The Kinsey Institute did not die with him, and continues its work. Though they are often tight-lipped, they are believed to have a collection of erotica that is second only to the Vatican's. Honestly. Selections were recently featured in an exhibition and book entitled *Peek*.

The Institute is not interested in walk-in guinea pig volunteers. Your best bet to see what they're working on now is to check out their Web site.

Morrison Hall, 1165 E. 3rd St. #302, Bloomington, IN 47405

(812) 855-7686

E-mail: kinsey@indiana.edu

Hours: Always visible; Tours bimonthly on Friday afternoons from 2:30 to 3:30, call for
   reservations

Cost: Free

www.indiana.edu/~kinsey

Directions: Five blocks east of Indiana Ave.

Rose Hill Cemetery, 4th & Elm Sts., Bloomington, IN 47404

(812) 349-3498

Hours: Daily 9 A.M.–5 P.M.

Cost: Free

Directions: Eight blocks west of College Ave. on 8th St.

BUDDHA
Outlaw **Sam Bass** was born southwest of Buddha on July 21, 1851.

BUTLERVILLE
Richard Nixon's mother, Hannah Milhous, was born 4.5 miles southeast of Butlerville in 1885. Her family moved to California in 1897. The home in which she was born burned down in December 1968, one month after Nixon was elected President.

CORRECT
The town name of Correct is incorrect. It was originally named Comet by its postmaster after Halley's Comet. But his handwriting was so poor, the head post office wrote down Correct.

Midwestern Tibet

Bloomington might seem an odd location for the focal point of Tibetan cultural activity in the United States, but the town has long been the home of Thubten Norbu, the Dalai Lama's brother and a retired IU professor. He opened the Tibetan Cultural Center in 1987, and the building was consecrated by his Nobel Peace Prize–winning sibling. The place has a Jangchub Chorten containing hair from the previous 13 Dalai Lamas, and to see their heads, well, that's quite an accomplishment.

Norbu's son, Jigme, runs one of the two Tibetan restaurants in Bloomington, the Snow Lion. (Most towns would be lucky to have just one!) And if you're thinking of developing a simpler lifestyle, there's always the Dagom Gaden Tensung Ling Monastery in Cascades Park. Do you look good in orange?

Tibetan Cultural Center, 3655 S. Snoddy Rd., PO Box 2581, Bloomington, IN 47402

(812) 334-7046

E-mail: tcc@tibetancc.com

Hours: Grounds: daily 9 A.M.–6 P.M.; Cultural Center, Sunday noon–3 P.M.

Cost: Free

www.tibetancc.com

Directions: Smith Rd. south to E. Rogers Rd., west to Snoddy Rd., south to the Center.

Dagom Gaden Tensung Ling Tibetan Buddhist Monastery, 102 Clubhouse Dr.,
Bloomington, IN 47404

(812) 339-0857

Hours: Daily 7 A.M.–8:30 P.M.

Cost: Free

www.ganden.org

Directions: Just west of Business 37, north of Rte. 45, in Cascades Park.

Snow Lion Restaurant, 113 S. Grant St., Bloomington, IN 47408

(812) 336-0835

Hours: Lunch, Monday–Friday 11:30 A.M.–2 P.M.; Dinner, daily 5–10 P.M.

Cost: Meals $6–$15

Directions: Four blocks east of College Ave. at 5th St.

Anyetsang's Little Tibet, 415 E. 4th St., Bloomington, IN 47408

(812) 331-0122

Hours: Daily 11 A.M.–10 P.M.

Cost: Meals $6–$15

Directions: One block west of Indiana Ave. at Dunn St.

Where's James?

Bruceville
Giant Peach

In the final pages of Roald Dahl's *James and the Giant Peach*, the enormous fruit tumbles from the skies over New York and is impaled on the antenna of the Empire State Building. The Giant Peach west of Bruceville missed a similar fate by a mere few feet.

Sitting beside a 40-foot yellow obelisk, the Giant Peach advertises a produce market on Rte. 41/150. It makes a perfect opportunity if you're traveling with somebody named James . . . or a gigantic talking grasshopper.

Home of the Big Peach, Rte. 41, Bruceville, IN 47516

(812) 324-2548

Hours: Always visible

Cost: Free

Directions: West of Bruceville, five miles north of Vincennes on the west side of the highway.

Mrs. Claus had too much eggnog.

Clarksville
Mad, Mad Mary Kay Lady

Madison Avenue executives take note: If you want to create an eye-catching advertisement on a limited budget, consider buying an old Cadillac, a few buckets of paint, and a store mannequin. That's what the owners of

Couch's Body Shop did, and they've been drawing in customers like flies.

Couch's buried the Caddy nose down along Blackiston Mill Road, painted it flamingo pink, and perched a female mannequin atop the back bumper. It's as if a drunken Mary Kay Lady had ditched her vehicle and was sitting around waiting for a tow truck. Depending on the season, she is clad in a different seasonal outfit. Mrs. Claus at Christmastime. A leggy leprechaun on St. Patrick's Day. Red, white, and blue for the Fourth of July. What does this have to do with what they're selling? Well, what other body shops do you see listed in a travel guide?

Couch's Body & Frame Shop, 2803 Blackiston Mill Rd., Clarksville, IN 47129

(812) 944-4044

Hours: Always visible

Cost: Free

Directions: Exit 4 from I-65 to Rte. 131 south, turn right on Blackiston Mill Rd. just after the Green Tree Mall, two miles north.

CORYDON
Indiana's only Civil War battle was fought in Corydon on July 9, 1863.

James Best, better known as Sheriff Roscoe P. Coltrain from *The Dukes of Hazzard*, was born in Corydon.

DALE
Actress **Florence Henderson** of the TV sitcom *The Brady Bunch*, was born in Dale on Valentine's Day 1934.

DILLSBORO
A UFO was spotted hovering over a Nike missile base near Dillsboro in the spring of 1966. Permission to fire on the craft was denied.

EPSOM
The town of Epsom was named for the water from its wells; it tasted like Epsom salts.

World's Second Largest Clock

Clarksville has long played third fiddle to neighboring Jeffersonville, Indiana, and Louisville, Kentucky, just across the river. Louisville has a baseball bat named after it; Jeffersonville has its famous steamboats—but neither of those towns have the World's Second Largest Clock. That's in Clarksville.

The Colgate Clock, shaped like a gigantic stop sign, is 40 feet in diameter. That's larger than London's Big Ben. Its hour hand is 16 feet long, its minute hand measures 20½ feet, and its pendulum weighs 330 pounds. The clock looms over the Colgate-Palmolive plant, housed in the former Indiana Reformatory for Men. It was moved here from another Colgate facility in New Jersey where (presumably) workers had a better on-time performance. Rather than have it face north, toward Clarksville, the clock faces south, toward Kentucky. During the summer the states don't share the same time zone, so in addition to bragging about their big-ass timepiece, they show everyone in Louisville that Clarksville is one hour younger.

S. Clark Blvd. & Woerner St., Clarksville, IN 47129

No phone

Hours: Always visible

Cost: Free

Directions: Just northwest of the I-65 bridge to Louisville, at the Ohio River.

Columbus
Birthplace of Corn Flakes

Columbus is mighty proud of its architectural legacy, and with good reason; few towns outside Chicago and New York have as many examples of modern architecture. But one building on the city's "significant building" tour stands out above all others, at least to breakfast lovers: the former "Mill A" at Fifth and Jackson. It was here, in the late 1870s, that James Vanoy invented corn flakes by accident. He named it Cerealine. Originally sold wholesale in 1880 for beer preparation, somebody realized the crunchy creation tasted good all by itself. In 1884 the nation got its first taste of corn flakes, sold by the newly formed American Hominy Company.

The mill was later converted into the headquarters of the Cummins

Engine Company. This manufacturer foots the bill for most of the innovative architecture in Columbus, known as "The Athens of the Midwest."

Cummins Engine Company, Cerealine Building, 5th & Jackson Sts., Columbus, IN 47202

Private phone

Hours: Always visible

Cost: Free

www.columbus.in.us

Directions: Two blocks east of Rte. 11, three blocks north of Rte. 7.

Dale
Dr. Ted's Musical Marvels

Somewhere between humankind's first drum and today's digital audio devices was a short-lived era of mechanical instruments. These music makers were not playback machines, like phonographs, but were constructed of recognizable instruments. Player pianos, music boxes, and calliopes are the most common "musical marvels," but hold onto your ears when you step into Ted Waflart's place.

Dr. Ted's museum contains some of the most elaborate mechanical instruments around, and what's more, he'll play them all for you on the 90-minute tour. The largest device, the "Decap" Belgian Dance Organ, was used in small European towns that couldn't afford an orchestra for their parties. The 24-foot-long contraption contains a 535-pipe organ, two saxophones, cymbals, tempo blocks, two accordions, drums, and more. Plug it in and get ready to boogie! Other machines, beautifully restored by Dr. Ted, bang out tunes controlled with air-driven valves, copper-coated rotating disks, and punched paper rolls. Who needs digital quality when you can have the real thing?

Rte. 231, R.R. 2, PO Box 30-A, Dale, IN 47523

(812) 937-4250

Hours: June–August, Monday–Saturday 10 A.M.–6 P.M., Sunday 1–6 P.M.; May, September, Saturday 10 A.M.–6 P.M., Sunday 1–6 P.M.

Cost: Adults $6, Seniors $5, Kids (6–12) $2

Directions: Half mile north of I-64, Exit 57, on Rte. 231.

Evansville
The Lady in Gray

Tales of ghosts in old buildings are not uncommon, but photographic "evidence" of these spirits is rare, and ghost-hunting Web-cams are almost unheard of. But not in Evansville.

The Lady in Gray has haunted this town's main library since 1936. Most believe her to be an old librarian. Others claim she's the spirit of Louise Carpenter, daughter of the collection's founder, Willard Carpenter, since ghosts often hang out where their living bodies experienced pain and suffering. Carpenter had every reason to be bitter toward the library for, as she saw it, her inheritance was gobbled up by this elaborate building and all its fancy books.

Luckily, the Lady in Gray is not a vengeful ghost. She likes to hang out near the Children's Room and the restrooms on the lower level. She's always dressed in a Victorian outfit . . . and it's gray. If patrons don't see her, they often experience "cold spots" or smell her perfume, which reminds many of patchouli. Could the Lady in Gray be a Deadhead, sneaking a little doobie between the racks? Some folks aim to find out.

A security camera once caught a glimpse of her wispy figure near the restrooms. Realizing she could be photographed, the *Evansville Courier & Press* set up a pair of ghost-cams, one in the main library and the other in the Children's Room. They snap a shot every 10 minutes during the day, at night the image refreshes every 30 seconds. Visitors to the Web site are encouraged to save and report anything suspicious, and you're welcome to view their findings, under "Proof!" Some of the obvious hoaxes are found under "Spoof!", such as the spooky appearances of Colonel Sanders, Kathy Lee Gifford, Pikachu, the Three Stooges, and numerous Teletubbies. According to the *Courier*, the Willard Library ghost-cam is one of the most visited Web-cams on the Internet . . . if you don't count "naked sorority" sites.

Willard Library, 21 First Ave., Evansville, IN 47710

(812) 425-4309

Hours: Monday–Tuesday 9 A.M.–8 P.M., Wednesday–Friday 9 A.M.–5:30 P.M., Saturday 9 A.M.–5 P.M., Sunday 1–5 P.M.

Cost: Free

www.courierpress.com/ghost

www.willard.lib.in.us

Directions: At the corner of First and Division Sts.

EVANSVILLE

Evansville claims to be the "Refrigeration Capital of the World" since, at one time, the town manufactured a fourth of the nation's refrigerators. A "Miss Refrigeradorable" was crowned for many years in an annual citywide beauty competition.

During a rainstorm on May 21, 1911, a two-foot alligator dropped from the sky onto the front stoop of Evansville resident Mrs. Hiram Winchell. She and several other women chased it into the bushes and killed it with bed slats.

Much of downtown Evansville sits atop a labyrinth of flooded coal mine shafts.

Residents of Evansville are called Evansvillians.

Actor **Ron Glass**, better known as Harris on *Barney Miller*, was born in Evansville on July 10, 1945.

An unknown creature grabbed the leg of a Dogtown woman, Mrs. Darwin Johnson, while she swam in the Ohio River near Evansville on August 21, 1955. The monster was scared off by her swimming companion, Mrs. Chris Lamble. The creature left a green, slimy handprint on her leg, which could not be washed off for several days.

Bobo, a white-throated capuchin monkey, lived at Evansville's Mesker Park Zoo from 1935 to 1981. When he died at age 53, he was the oldest living monkey in captivity.

One reason bachelor parties hire strippers today.

Gosport
The Chivalry Trough

Long before American bachelor parties became opportunities to embarrass and blackmail new grooms with strippers on videotape, prewedding customs were a bit more down to earth. In the town of Gosport, it was a tradition for friends to toss a soon-to-be hubby into a 8 x 4-foot concrete ditch filled with cold water. The dunking place was dubbed the Chivalry Trough, and the whole process was a symbolic welcome into the cold, hard reality of matrimony.

As fun as it was, the practice eventually faded away. Today, the Chivalry Trough can be found among the weeds, near the railroad trestle, by the ruins of the old Brewer Flour Mill. Be advised that if you want to resurrect a dunking for old time's sake, there are serious risks. The trough is empty and surrounded by poison ivy, and all the groomsmen could end up with a nasty rash. How do you explain *that* on your wedding night?

North St., Gosport, IN 47433

No phone

Hours: Always visible

Cost: Free

Directions: Follow North St., which runs parallel to Main St., one block north, east until it goes down the hill. On the left, at the bend are four pillars, and on the right, in the weeds, is the Chivalry Trough.

FLORENCE

Florence was once home to the Anti-Swearing Society. Members fined one another for uttering profanities.

FREETOWN

While working as a technician for Indiana Bell (and before becoming famous), **John Cougar Mellencamp** accidentally cut off phone service to all of Freetown.

FRENCH LICK

Born December 7, 1956, **Larry Bird** (also known as "The Hick from French Lick"), first played basketball at Spring Valley High School (326 S. Larry Bird Blvd.), graduating in 1974. You can find hometown Bird souvenirs at the French Lick Five and Dime (469 Maple St.).

A monster dubbed Fluorescent Freddie was spotted in the woods near the French Lick Airport (9764 W. Country Rd. 375S), three miles south of town, in March 1965. He had glowing red eyes and a shimmering green coat.

HENRYVILLE

Colonel Harland Sanders was *not* born in Kentucky, but Henryville, Indiana, on September 9, 1890.

JASONVILLE

The town of Jasonville was once headed by a professional Elvis impersonator, Bruce Borders. His motto was "By day the Mayor, by night . . . THE KING!"

Hindustan
Don't Sit in the Witch's Chair!

Most people can recall an urban legend from their high school days about a local cemetery and a curse associated with it. The story of the Witch's Chair is one of those tales.

The dead buried in Stepp Cemetery were from a religious sect called the Crabbites. They were snake-handling fundamentalists and practitioners of free love—not a typical congregation. While the sex might have attracted converts, the poisonous vipers kept the congregation limited.

One follower, a young woman named Anna, had a baby who was tragically killed by a hit-and-run driver on old Route 37. The mother buried her daughter in this rural graveyard, but returned every night to exhume the girl's body and cradle it in her arms. Not long after she began her nocturnal activities, a tree near the grave was struck by lightning. The smoking stump made a fine chair for the nutty, grieving mom. She always dressed in black and could be seen most nights, rocking back and forth, on what became known as the Witch's Chair.

This "witch" didn't live forever, but the curse that claimed her child lingers on. According to legend, anyone who sits in her chair during a full moon will die, one year to the day after the brazen act. Not much is left of the old cemetery but a few tombstones and a lot of empty beer cans. Several old stumps could be chairs, but none look very comfortable. That alone should be reason enough not to test fate.

Stepp Cemetery, Morgan-Monroe State Forest, Old State Highway 37, Hindustan, IN 47401

(765) 342-4026

Hours: Daily 8 A.M.–7 P.M.

Cost: Free

www.state.in.us/dnr/forestry/property/morgmonr.htm

Directions: In the park, follow the trail leading away from the curved stone wall along old Rte. 37, just west of the Shady Pines Picnic Area.

JASPER

Jasper is "The Town That Made Garbage Illegal." Garbage collection was discontinued on August 1, 1950, when sink waste disposals were installed in every home.

Just the tip of the geode-berg.

Jasper
Geode Garden

It's easy to find a simple grotto built alongside an old Catholic church in the Midwest. But the Geode Garden in Jasper? When did the builders decide enough was enough?

The garden stretches for two city blocks and contains dozens of statue-filled niches lumped together in several areas. Most of the pedestals, fences, fountains, pillars, light posts, and benches are encrusted with unsplit geodes, making the whole structure look like a collection of carefully arranged popcorn balls.

Bartley St., Jasper, IN 47546

No phone

Hours: Always visible

Cost: Free

Directions: Two blocks due west of the St. Joseph's Cathedral on Rte. 231, between 9th and 11th Sts.

Southern Indiana, with its rich limestone geology, is also rich in caves. For true spelunkers, there are plenty of undeveloped caverns to explore. For those tourists who don't want to spend their time crawling through bat guano for the thrill of falling down a bottomless pit, there are several options to consider. Here are four of the region's best-known caves.

BEDFORD: BLUESPRING CAVERNS

White River tributaries have carved an underground wonderland where blind albino fish and crawdads thrive. They look like George Hamilton . . . without the tanning bed. Visitors to Bluespring Caverns take a Mystery River Voyage in an electric boat through 4,000 feet of flooded passage-ways, the longest navigable "lost river" in the nation. This place is cool—52° Fahrenheit, to be exact.

Bluespring Caverns were discovered in the 1940s by farmer George Colglazier. A pond on his farm drained overnight and, since his livestock didn't seem particularly thirsty, he figured something must be going on below his feet. He was right. Cavers continue to find more passageways; recent discoveries indicate that this hole in the ground is one of the 10 largest in the world.

Bluespring Cavern Rd., R.R. 11, PO Box 1245, Bedford, IN 47421
(812) 279-9471
E-mail: jar45@aol.com
Hours: June–August, daily 9 A.M.–5 P.M.; April–May, September–October,
  Saturday– Sunday 9 A.M.–5 P.M.
Cost: Adults $10, Kids (3–15) $5
Directions: Five miles southwest of town on Rte. 50, west on County Road 450S
  to Bluespring Cavern Rd.

CORYDON: SQUIRE BOONE CAVERNS AND VILLAGE

Squire Boone and his older brother, Daniel, found this southern Indiana cavern in 1790 while exploring the region, and while Daniel went on to bigger and better things, Squire settled down and built a grist mill in 1804. Though he made his living aboveground, Boone spent his free time exploring the hole under his place.

Boone loved his cave so much he requested to be buried there, and in 1815 he got his final wish. Nobody kept track of where his body was interred, so when human bones were unearthed in 1974, everyone assumed they'd found the cavern's namesake. The remains were placed in a walnut casket along the underground walkway, unburied and chilled to a constant 54°F, which is where you can see them today.

But that's not all. Squire Boone Caverns is more "active" than most caves. Blind, albino crawfish live in an underground river flowing past the cave's stalactites and stalagmites. Can you see them? They can't see you!

Rte. 135 South, PO Box 411, Corydon, IN 47112
(812) 732-4381 or (502) 425-CAVE
E-mail: spelunk@squireboone.com
Hours: June–August, daily 10 A.M.–6 P.M., tours every 30 minutes; September–
   December, March–May, 10 A.M., noon, 2 P.M., 4 P.M. tours; January–February,
   Saturday–Sunday 10 A.M., noon, 2 P.M., 4 P.M. tours
Cost: Adults $11, Kids (6–11) $6.50
www.squireboonecaverns.com
Directions: Ten miles south of town on Rte. 135, left on Squire Boone Caverns Rd.

MARENGO: MARENGO CAVE

If you're looking for stalactites and stalagmites, Marengo Cave is your best bet in Indiana. Other caverns have larger "rooms," albino critters, and boating trips; but this is the only place to find formations like the Crystal Palace, the Prison Bars, Candlestick Park, the Lion's Cage, the Pipe Organ, and the ever-popular Pulpit Rock, where dozens of spelunkers have tied the knot.

Marengo Cave was discovered in 1883 by two children and is a National Historic Landmark. Every year the caves host a "marathon" run down the Dripstone Trail. The toughest aspect of the run is dodging stone outcroppings in the near darkness. The easiest part is jogging along a comfortable 54°F track.

Marengo Cave Rd., PO Box 217, Marengo, IN 47140
(812) 365-2705
E-mail: blueriver@otherside.com
Hours: June–August, daily 9 A.M.–6 P.M.; September–May, daily 9:30 A.M.–5 P.M.
Cost: Adults $11–$16, Kids (4–12) $5.50–$8 (depending on the tour)
www.marengocave.com
Directions: Just north of town off Rte. 64.

WYANDOTTE: WYANDOTTE CAVE

Last, but certainly not least, is Wyandotte Cave, home of Monument Mountain and the tallest stalagmite in the world: the Pillar of the Constitution! Monument Mountain towers 185 feet inside Rothrock Cathedral, but still has a way to go before touching the 200-foot high ceiling. Give it a few million years. This cave has five different levels and includes places like the Hill of Humility, the Valley of the Shades, Bandit's Hall, Cleopatra's Palace, the Crater Room, and the Senate Chamber. Wyandotte Cave claims to be the third oldest cave in the nation, with 23 miles of caves yet to be explored.

7315 S. Wyandotte Cave Rd., Wyandotte, IN 47137

(812) 738-2782

E-mail: hcwc@theremc.com

Hours: June–September, daily 9 A.M.–5 P.M.; October–May, Tuesday–Sunday
9 A.M.–5 P.M.

Cost: Adults $5–$15, Kids $3–$6 (depending on the tour)

www.cccn.net/wwcomp.htm#wc

Directions: Just north of Rte. 62 on Wyandotte Cave Rd.

Jeffersonville
The Bridge That Goes Nowhere

The present nickname of this structure, the Bridge That Goes Nowhere, is not intended as a slam against the towns on either end. It really does go nowhere.

The Big Four Bridge was constructed in the early 1890s to carry the Cleveland, Cincinnati, Chicago & St. Louis Railroad over the Ohio River. The span opened in 1895 after numerous deadly construction accidents killed 61 laborers. Those deaths made the crash of two interurban trains on the bridge in January 1918 almost a footnote; only 20 riders died in that mishap.

Time and other bridges eventually took their toll on the Big Four Bridge. When the interurbans stopped running, the tracks on both sides of the bridge were removed, isolating the span from both towns.

Louisville has kicked around the idea of rebuilding its access ramp and erecting a casino, mall, or something else on the old deck, over the water. Who knows, the Bridge That Goes Nowhere might go somewhere again.

Big Four Bridge, Mulberry St., Jeffersonville, IN 47131

No phone

Hours: Always visible

Cost: Free

Directions: Just east of the I-65 bridge, at the Ohio River.

Howard Steamboat Museum

The paddlewheel steamboat was a powerful force in American history, yet it is all but extinct today, save for riverboat casinos that rarely leave shore. At the Howard Steamboat Museum you can explore the legacy of these floating hotels where many of them first touched the water.

James Howard launched his Jeffersonville operations in 1834 at the dawn of the steamboat age. He was 19 years old at the time. The operation grew at a breakneck pace, to the point where half the flat-bottom sidewheelers on the western rivers had been built in the Howard Shipyards. James Howard died here in 1876; the 62-year-old underestimated his final jump onto a departing steamboat, fell into the Ohio River, and drowned. But the Howard family carried on his work until 1941 when the yards were sold to the U.S. Navy at the outset of World War II. Workers then built LSTs, sub chasers, and other oceangoing craft to aid in the effort. Today, the shipyards operate under the name of Jeffboat.

You'll learn all the details, and much more, at a museum housed in the 1894 Howard Mansion. The ornate structure was built by the shipyard's craftsmen and, if it had a couple of paddlewheels and was painted white, might be mistaken for a ship run aground. The ground floor has been restored to its original, turn-of-the-century appearance following a fire in the 1970s. The second floor contains dozens of steamboat models and items salvaged from the *Robert E. Lee*, the *Natchez*, and others. These beautiful crafts could float in only 18 inches of water and achieve speeds of 40 knots. On the museum's top floor is an exhibit of the WWII boats built here, focusing on the LST landing craft used during the D-Day invasion. Look around the museum and you'll find a few odd items, including a wooden typewriter and the original 22-ton paddlewheel shaft from the *Delta Queen*.

1101 E. Market St., PO Box 606, Jeffersonville, IN 47131

(812) 283-3728

Hours: Tuesday–Saturday 10 A.M.–3 P.M., Sunday 1–3 P.M.

Cost: Adults $4, Seniors (65+) $3, Teens (9–18) $2, Kids (6–9) $1

www.steamboatmuseum.org

Directions: Thirteen blocks northeast of the I-65 bridge, along the Ohio River.

Leopold
Thou Shalt Not Steal

By all accounts, the Civil War's Andersonville Prison Camp in Georgia was no picnic. Disease. Starvation. Packs of man-eating bloodhounds. It was in this "maniac's nightmare" that three Union prisoners from Indiana, Lambert Rogier, Henry Devillez, and Isidore Naviaux, pledged to honor the Virgin Mary if they survived the ordeal, even if it meant *stealing*.

The trio made it home and, in 1867, Rogier set sail for Luxembourg, his eyes on Our Lady of Consolation. The statue he sought was carved in 1628 for Father Broquart, a priest who, having made a similar pact with the Mother of God, miraculously survived a bubonic plague outbreak in Europe. Rogier made a copy of the centuries-old statue, then swapped it with the original.

Many in Indiana today deny Rogier did anything but make a copy the statue, but the original's owners asked King Leopold to intercede on their behalf. When the King learned the statue had ended up in a burg that shared his name, he calmed the nerves of the finger-pointers and the whole issue was swept under the rug.

The statue remains in Leopold today. Depending on the season, Our Lady of Consolation is dressed in a variety of liturgical outerwear, sort of like a holy Barbie. The baby Jesus sits in her outstretched hand. A marble replica of the statue stands outside the church, but the original is locked up at night . . . for good reason.

Shrine of Our Lady of Consolation, St. Augustine Church, General Delivery, Leopold, IN 47551

(812) 843-5143

Hours: Daily 9 A.M.–6 P.M.

Cost: Free

Directions: On the south side of town, at the corner of St. Augustine and Lafayette Sts.

Lincoln City
Don't Drink the Milk!

Mother always told you, "Drink your milk!" Well, Mom wasn't always right. Take Abe Lincoln's mother, Nancy Hanks Lincoln; she perished on the family farm on October 5, 1818, the victim of "milk sickness."

While not understood at the time, "milk sickness" should have been called "milk poisoning." It was sometimes called "puking sickness" or "the trembles." During times of drought, cattle would eat plants they would normally avoid, one of them being the white snakeroot. Toxins from this plant accumulated in the tissues of the animals and passed through their milk. If a person drank too much of that milk, it wasn't pretty: vomiting, muscle pain, constipation, coma, and death.

The Lincolns had moved to Indiana in 1816 to escape land title disputes in Kentucky, and now, two years later, Abe's mother was dead. He was only nine years old. His father, Thomas, married a second time, to a woman Abe would come to feel was his mother, Sarah Bush Johnston. The family abandoned their Hoosier farm for Illinois in 1830.

Today you'll find a reconstructed homestead. The locations of the cabin and Nancy's grave are approximate. There is a bronzed sill and hearthstone believed to be part of the original cabin, and an elaborate tombstone rests atop a hill where Nancy was buried. Adjoining the farm is a visitors center and museum.

Lincoln Boyhood National Memorial, Rte. 162, PO Box 1816, Lincoln City, IN 47552

(812) 937-4541

E-mail: LIBO_Superintendent@nps.gov

Hours: Daily 8 A.M.–5 P.M.

Cost: Adults $2, Kids free

www.nps.gov/libo

Directions: Four miles west of Santa Claus on Rte. 162.

LOOGOOTEE

The name Loogootee is the mutant combination of two early residents: Lowe and Gootee.

Heaven for clowns. Hell for the rest of us.

Martinsville
Clown Heaven

If you are one of those people who find clowns unsettling, perhaps you should come to this bright yellow shop on a lonely road near Martinsville: Clown Heaven. This is not where a bunch of harp-strumming Bozos try to cram as many as possible onto a small cloud. It is a place where living, breathing clowns can join together to swap pie stories and squirt one another with plastic lapel flowers.

If you harbor a secret desire to wear a red nose, rainbow wig, and shoes that are 27 sizes too large, come on by Clown Heaven and act on your impulses. Clown Heaven conducts 10-week courses where you will be made up in at least three different faces, learn the basics of balloon sculpture and magic, and participate in skits designed to bring out your inner clown. If you're lucky, maybe somebody will squirt some seltzer down your pants.

4782 Old State Road 37S, Martinsville, IN 46151

(765) 342-6888

Hours: Thursday–Friday 11 A.M.–7 P.M., Saturday 10 A.M.–2 P.M.

Cost: Free; clown classes $80 for 10 weeks

Directions: Rte. 37 south to Old Rte. 37, three miles south of town.

Touuuuuuuuuch them!
Photo by author, courtesy of C. R. Schiefer

The Touchables Sculpture Garden

Go ahead, touuuuuuch them! Stroke. Caress. Explore—that's why these works of art are here. To listen to sculptor C. R. Schiefer describe his art, there is no way to fully appreciate the pieces until you put your hands all over them. There are more than 150 figures scattered over a 10-acre outdoor "gallery," so it'll take you a while to grope them all. Quite a few are anatomically correct—so enjoy yourself!

Schiefer spent a quarter century working as a speech pathologist before he discovered, just by chance, his talent for carving. As the years rolled by, he developed a style, focusing heavily on the human form and images from native cultures around the world. He also enjoys carving animals, many of which can be seen along the shores of a holding pond on his land.

The entrance to the Touchables Sculpture Garden is marked by a large piece called *Population 999*: three stacked blocks covered with 999 faces. Respectful guests are welcome to wander the property during daylight hours, but be forewarned, there are 1,998 eyes trained on your every move.

5270 Low Gap Rd., Martinsville, IN 46151

(765) 342-6211

E-mail: schiefer@scican.net

Hours: Always visible

Cost: Free

www.scican/~sciefer

Directions: Southeast of town on Mahalasville Rd. three miles, turn right (south) on Low Gap Rd. for three miles, on the right, south of Downey Rd. (County Road 525).

MEDORA
Medora's name was derived from three musical notes, do, re, and mi, sung out of order.

NEW ALBANY
A tornado in 1917 killed more than 50 New Albany residents.

NEWBURGH
On July 18, 1862, Newburgh was the first town north of the Mason-Dixon line to be captured by the Confederate Army during the Civil War.

Fun times in Milltown.

Milltown
Shoe Tree

Do you have an old pair of sneakers in your laundry room, but don't have the heart to throw them *out*? Well, bring them to Milltown and throw them *up* . . . into a tree!

Nobody is sure who started it, but 25 years ago, shoes were spotted hanging from the branches of a white oak at the intersection of two gravel roads south of town. Soon it became the most exciting thing to do in

Milltown—take off your footwear and toss them in the air! (If you've been to Milltown, you know this is still the case.)

Here's the trick to successful shoe tossing: tie the laces together with some length, heave the pair in a pinwheel motion, and pray they tangle with any of the 1,000+ pairs already dangling above.

County Roads 23 & 30, Milltown, IN 47145

No phone

Hours: Always visible

Cost: Free

Directions: Five miles south of town on County Road 23, at the intersection with County Road 30.

World's Largest Condom Model.

Mitchell
Virgil I. Grissom State Memorial

Can a kid from a small town in Indiana grow up to be an astronaut? You betcha! And not just any astronaut, but the second American to break the gravitational bonds of Earth. Virgil "Gus" Grissom would also go on to command the first Gemini mission and die in a tragic launch pad fire on Apollo I.

Grissom was born here on April 3, 1926, and attended Riley Elementary. That school later burned to the ground, but bricks from the structure were saved and later used to build a low wall around a 44-foot limestone rocket erected on the same site.

As a pilot in the Korean War, Grissom earned a Distinguished Flying Cross and the chance to be a test pilot/astronaut in the upstart space program. Piloting *Liberty Bell 7* on July 21, 1961, his career almost sank with the capsule at splashdown. Though evidence later proved him blameless, the event plagued him until long after the event. It is no coincidence that the craft he piloted on his second space flight, Gemini I, was nicknamed the *Unsinkable Molly Brown*. The former pilot was chosen to command the first moon mission, but died with the rest of his crew in a freak fire on January 27, 1967.

Much of the world's Grissom-abilia is located in a memorial museum outside Mitchell. You'll see the space suit and helmet he wore on the ill-fated Mercury mission, the Gemini capsule he piloted on March 23, 1965, Norman Rockwell's painting of Gus in his Apollo flight suit, and personal items from his Indiana childhood.

Redstone Rocket Memorial, 6th & College Sts., Mitchell, IN 47446

No phone

Hours: Always visible

Cost: Free

Directions: Next to the Mitchell Municipal Building, five blocks north of Rte. 60, one
    block west of the railroad tracks.

Virgil I. Grissom Memorial, Spring Mill State Park, Rte. 60, PO Box 376, Mitchell,
    IN 47446

(812) 849-4129

Hours: Daily 8:30 A.M.–4 P.M.; Park: daily 7 A.M.–11 P.M.

Cost: In-state $3, out-of-state $5

www.state.in.us/dnr/parklake/parks/springmill.html

Directions: Three miles east of town on Rte. 60 to the park entrance, just to the right of
    the main gate.

Morgantown
Rock House Inn

When James "Smith" Knight dreamed of a home for his new family in 1894, he did what today is called "thinking outside the box." He built the outer surface of the 10-room home with concrete blocks, into which he embedded anything he could get his hands on. Though he mostly used small stones, if you look long enough, you can also find broken dishes, marbles, geodes, shells, dolls' heads, a boar's skull, and more sticking out of the siding. Knight fashioned his name out of lumps of coal placed over the front door, and included his wife Isabelle on another panel. She died 23 years later and Knight eventually remarried. Knight fathered 20 children between both marriages, and died in 1934.

The building is in remarkable shape for being more than a century old. Today the Rock House Inn is a bed-and-breakfast that can accommodate a dozen guests in its six bedrooms.

380 W. Washington St., PO Box 10, Morgantown, IN 46160

(812) 597-5100

Hours: Always available

Cost: $80–$95/night

Directions: Just east of the intersection of Rtes. 135 & 252 (Washington St.).

The pharaohs didn't give up so easily.

Needmore
Cursed Pyramid and Crumbling Wall of China

The limestone used to build the Empire State Building was excavated from the Empire Quarry near Bedford, the "Limestone Capital of the World." Stone from the region was also used to construct the Pentagon and Washington's National Cathedral; New York's Cathedral of St. John the Divine, Rockefeller Center, and Radio City Music Hall; Chicago's Tribune Tower and Merchandise Mart; and the University of Moscow. That's quite a resume.

But then, like the prideful folk of Babel, the quarries of Bedford overreached. They planned to build a 1/5 scale, eight-story model of the Pyramid of Cheops, and a 650-foot segment of the Great Wall of China. The promoters intended to demonstrate the skills of local stonecutters, to inject a little life into the local economy, and perhaps touch the face of God.

Who was paying for it? You! After the project received $700,000 in federal funds, construction began. Soon legislators bowed to pressure to cut off the pork barrel project, and the bankroll vanished like a desert mirage. Two pyramid-topped columns mark the entrance to this now abandoned boondoggle. Follow the road for a half mile and you'll find the remains of the pyramid's base among the weeds.

Limestone Tourist Park, Needmore, IN 47421

No phone

Hours: Always visible

Cost: Free

Directions: Take Trogden Rd. east off Rte. 37, keep bearing right as you pass through
  town, take a right at the "T" and follow the road until it ends with boulders in the road.

New Albany
Yenawine Exhibit

After retiring from his job on the railroad at the age of 60, Merle Yenawine vowed to keep busy. Drawing from his childhood experiences, Yenawine began creating dioramas of rural life in southern Indiana. What made his 60 scenes unique was that his figures moved, controlled from beneath by small motors and machinery. Yenawine would bring his creations around to local schools for the kids to enjoy, and when he grew too old to do that, sold most of the collection to the NA-FC School Corporation for $800. It was later purchased by the Carnegie Center and put on permanent display. The enormous body of work has 475 different moving objects, all of which can be activated by buttons on their display cases.

Yenawine's scenes are humorous and action-packed. Two men fight near an outhouse in the Shotgun Wedding diorama. Kids misbehave in the One Room Schoolhouse. Ducks dance on the Family Farm. Reluctant pigs battle with farmers in the bloody Community Butchering—and who can blame them? The Town Carnival has a woman waltzing with bears, geese on a teeter-totter, ax throwers, and acrobats atop high poles. If you'd like to see how these contraptions function, the Main Street exhibit has a floor-level mirror to reflect the mechanics beneath the scene.

Carnegie Center for Art & History, 201 E. Spring St., New Albany, IN 47150

(812) 944-7336

Hours: Tuesday–Saturday 10 A.M.–5:30 P.M.

Cost: Free

carnegie.nafcpl.lib.in.us/exhibition.html

Directions: At the corner of Spring and Bank St., east of Rte. 64/150.

New Harmony
The Angel Gabriel's Footprints

A long, long, time ago, the Archangel Gabriel stood on a flat stone to blow his holy horn, and when he stepped off, his footprints were indelibly etched into the rock. Hard to believe, unless you are the type of person who would willingly follow a Lutheran visionary into the malaria-ridden swamps of southern Indiana.

That's what the folks of the Harmony Society did in 1814, so tales of a rock-stomping angel made as much sense as anything. A biblical Grauman's Theater? Sure—why not? Rapp told them the rock was from the Holy Land, but in actuality, he purchased the carved limestone in St. Louis.

The true story, when it got out, didn't sit too well with the folk who remained in New Harmony; but it didn't bother them so much that they tossed out the fake. Instead, it ended up in the backyard of the Rapp-Maclure House. Today, both home and footprints are protected by a high wall and fence. Historic New Harmony claims the site will one day be open to the public. But when will that be? The Second Coming? Why all the security? Could those tootsie tracks be real?

Rapp-Maclure Home, c/o Historic New Harmony, PO Box 579, New Harmony, IN 47631

(800) 231-2168 or (812) 682-4488

Hours: Always visible

Cost: Free

www.newharmony.org

Directions: At the corner of Main (Rte. 69) & Church (Rte. 66) Sts.

New Harmony Labyrinth

Lutheran separatist George Rapp had his own ideas about how the world worked, and he convinced 1,000 "Harmonists" (sometimes called Rappites) to leave rural Pennsylvania and follow him to Indiana in 1814. Their experiment became known as Harmonie, "That Wonder in the Wilderness." Rapp had his followers use their time constructively while waiting for Christ's return: clearing land, building homes, brewing beer, distilling whiskey. After 10 years and no Jesus, they packed their bags and headed back to Pennsylvania. The whole operation was sold to utopian Robert Owen for $150,000 in 1825.

Christening the failing enterprise "New Harmony," Owen revamped the commune with a socialist philosophy, and the place thrived as the cultural center of the Midwest prior to the Civil War. New Harmony slowly faded over the next century until an influx of cash in the 1980s helped spruce it up into a tourist trap.

Part of restoring this community was rebuilding the New Harmony Labyrinth, originally laid out by Rapp. This hedge maze was intended to represent the path of life: twisted and difficult. Because there are no dead ends or alternative paths, you're bound to end up in the center if you walk long enough. Apparently, at the end of our lives, we'll end up at a dinky shack. Streets of gold? Hardly!

Historic New Harmony, PO Box 579, New Harmony, IN 47631

(800) 231-2168 or (812) 682-4488

Hours: Always visible

Cost: Free

www.newharmony.evansville.net

Directions: At the south end of town on Main St. (Rte. 69).

ODON

In April 1941, a home near Odon was plagued by fires that popped up everywhere: inside a wall, under a bedspread, in pair of overalls hanging on a door, between pages of a book inside a closed drawer. Twenty-eight fires broke out in a single day.

Ya big Palooka!

Oolitic
A Big Palooka

Boxer Joe Palooka represented many American values: honesty, integrity, and punching an opponent's light out. It was only appropriate that he be honored on the face of Mt. Rushmore; and, if you've followed his comic strip since the 1940s, you know he was, right up there with the presidents.

But then the federal government got involved and Joe's square-jawed mug was blasted from the national monument, leaving only Washington, Jefferson, Lincoln, and Roosevelt. No Palooka.

It hardly seemed fair to the folks in limestone country, who had it in their power to recarve the character's image, albeit on a smaller scale. George Hitchcock, Sr. created a new monument in 1947, a full figure, right down to Joe's boxing trunks. It was erected in a ceremony attended by "Ham" Fisher, the comic strip's creator, in June 1948. Due to vandalism from some good-for-nothin' kids, the statue was bounced around the area, until it ended up outside the Oolitic Town Hall, where it stands today. He still has those six-pack abs, but his rib cage sticks out like a runway model's. Hey Joe, put some meat on those bones!

Town Hall, Main St., Oolitic, IN 47451

No phone

Hours: Always visible

Cost: Free

Directions: On Main St. between Lafayette and Hoosier Sts.

Orangeville
The Lost River and the Orangeville Rise

Somewhere near Route 337, eight miles due east of Orangeville, the Lost River lives up to its name and disappears into the earth. After meandering through 22 miles of subterranean caverns and passing beneath the village of Lost River, it pops back to the surface at a large spring called the Orangeville Rise.

To geologists, the location of this below-ground activity is known as the Karst Region, and unique as it is, there's a group dedicated to its preservation: The Karst Conservancy, PO Box 2401, Indianapolis, IN 46206. They successfully lobbied to have the Orangeville Rise designated a Registered Natural Landmark in 1975.

Center of town, Orangeville, IN 47452

No phone

Hours: Always visible

Cost: Free

Directions: Head north of Rte. 150 on the first road east of the Rte. 145 intersection to Orangeville, follow the signs.

Look out! Santa's shooting the naughty kids!

Pumpkin Center
The Museum of All Sorts of Stuff

Add Gray didn't believe in throwing anything away. ANYTHING. Though he was a pack rat, he wasn't a slob, as his widow, Mabel, points out while she walks you through the Museum of All Sorts of Stuff. Gray's legacy truly lives up to its name, because there doesn't seem to be any rhyme or reason to this collection, except that everything in it amused or interested Gray at one point in time.

The junk has been collected in an old general store/home/garage that seems to run on forever. Gray opened for business on October 31, 1922, and the museum has been operating ever since. Farm tools, license plates, and road signs hang from every rafter. Wagons, scales, and undertakers' baskets clutter the floors. And everywhere you look you see signs that read "Not responsible for accidents." Hmmmmm, better not touch anything.

Helpful signs explain it all for the city slicker. "Old barber chair owned by Sol Boone and traded to Lewis Rutherford for a 1924 Ford." "Chain and ankle cuffs from the old Paoli Jail." "Still over 100 yrs. old used in Taylor, Green & Larue Co. Ky in the mountains" . . . and the still has a moonshine recipe, too! Be sure to ask Mabel to turn on the mechanical sign featuring Santa and his gunslinging friend. Pulled by an elaborate system of strings and wires, the pair appear to be hunting while a cacophony of bells ring to flush the birds out of the bushes.

One final note, DO NOT make the mistake of calling this three-house town Pumpkin Center, despite what you read on the maps. Mabel Gray has lived here longer than any of those fancy map makers, and it's Punkin Center. Yesterday. Today. Forever.

243 Tater Rd., Pumpkin Center, IN 47452

Private phone

Hours: "Most days"

Cost: Free

Directions: Head southeast from Orleans on Rte. 337, turn south on County Rd. 500E
   (Tater Rd.).

PIKES PEAK

The town of Pikes Peak was named after a cold-footed local, James Ward, who turned back at the Ohio River on his way to the Colorado Gold Rush of 1859. Other residents would tease the store owner for years, labeling his establishment "Pikes Peak," and the name stuck.

Santa Claus
Holiday World

If you think Walt Disney came up with the concept of the theme park, think again. More than a decade before the Magic Kingdom opened its doors, Santa Claus Land welcomed Christmas-loving tourists. The year was 1946, and the park was more of a kiddie land than anything else. Over time it expanded, forming three "worlds": Christmas, for the tykes; Fourth of July, with carnival rides; and Halloween, with two roller coasters and a few other thrill rides. The Raven roller coaster, which roars through the wooded hills, was recently voted by enthusiasts as the best wooden roller coaster in the nation.

Purists needn't worry the place has "taken the Christ out of Christmas," for there's a concrete nativity scene just inside the gate where you can pose as a Wise Man in your "I'm with Stupid" T-shirt. The Hoosier Celebration Theater offers daily gospel performances of "Hallelujah!" And don't forget the park's mascot, Holidog—he's in the Bible *somewhere*, isn't he?

The newest addition to Holiday World is the Splashin' Safari water park. The slides have jungle names, not reindeer names. Perhaps the park was worried that a North Pole theme might freeze out potential guests.

Holiday World, PO Box 179, Santa Claus, IN 47579

(800) GO-SANTA (467-2682) or (812) 937-4401

Hours: May–October, hours vary, call ahead

Cost: Adults $26.95, Seniors (60+) $20.95, Kids (under 54") $20.95; prices lower for late-entry and off-season

www.holidayworld.com

Directions: Exit 63 from I-64, at the junction on Rtes. 162 and 245.

Santa Claus Town

There's no need to drive to the North Pole to hang out with Santa—come to southern Indiana! This small town was named (according to legend) by a confused child on Christmas Eve, 1852. Citizens were meeting in a local church to discuss what to call their town. Their first choice, Santa Fe, was already taken by another Indiana burg. Outside, a snowstorm blanketed the countryside and a sleigh approached the church. Hearing the jingle bells, a young girl shouted out, "Santa Claus!" and the town got its

DEDICATED
TO THE CHILDREN OF THE WORLD
IN
MEMORY OF AN UNDYING LOVE
DEC 25 1935   Carl A Barrett

Don't make me get the lumps of coal!

name. (Some reports of the meeting claim the adults had been drinking during the long meeting and were "ready for anything.")

This town's enthusiasm for all things Christmassy hasn't waned. In fact, many otherwise normal homes and businesses have been modified to look like castles and elf huts. They sit along cutely named streets like Candy Cane Lane, Sled Run, Noel Street, Ornament Lane, Chestnut by the Fire, Prancer Drive, Silver Bell Street, and Three Kings. New developments have branched out into other holidays, like Good Friday Boulevard, Easter Circle, and New Year's Eve Road. The town's fire truck is named Rudolph and has a red light on its "nose."

For the best Santa photo, check out the 22-foot, 40-ton granite Santa on the outskirts of town. This statue was erected in 1935 and is dedicated to all the children of the world, even those who don't believe in the jolly fellow.

Santa Claus Statue, Santa Claus, IN 47579
No phone
Hours: Always visible
Cost: Free
Directions: Just southwest of the intersection of Rtes. 245 & 162, on the east side of town

Each December the Santa Claus post office (the only one in the nation!) will cancel your cards with a special verse. But clearly, if you go to this much additional trouble sending out a photocopied family newsletter, you've got problems.

Santa Claus Post Office, Santa Claus, IN 47579
(812) 937-4469
Hours: Monday–Friday 7:30 A.M.–12:30 P.M., 1:30–4 P.M., Saturday 8:30–11:30 A.M.
Cost: Free
Directions: On Rte. 162/245 in the center of town.

If you want to make your yuletide visit to Santa Claus complete, spend a night at Santa's Lodge, just west of Holiday World. This lakeside hotel is decorated in green and red and has a year-round Christmas tree. Get blitzed in Blitzen's Bar. Pose with the many statues of Kris Kringle on the lawn. It's a yuletidal wave! Too bad the place isn't staffed with elves.

Santa's Lodge & St. Nick's Restaurant, 91 W. Rte. 162, PO Box 193, Santa Claus, IN 47579
(800) 640-7895 or (812) 937-1902
Hours: Always open
Cost: $40–$80/night
Directions: At the west end of town.

And if you're the Grinchy type, you might want to visit a special location on the northwest end of town: the Santa Claus Cemetery. Ho, oh no!

Santa Claus Cemetery, Rte. 245, Santa Claus, IN 47579

No phone

Hours: Always visible

Cost: Free

Directions: Northwest of the Rte. 245 intersection with Rte. 162, just past the United
  Methodist Church on Rte. 245.

Seymour
America's First Train Robbery

The Reno family was filled with bad 'uns. Ask the folks of Rockford, just north of Seymour. During the 1850s the town was plagued by a series of mysterious fires, leveling Rockford one building at a time. Each time a property was torched, another Reno clan member appeared and bought the charred land to build something new. This continued until five of every six properties in town were Reno-owned. Some of the more ambitious male family members formed the Reno Gang and terrorized southern Indiana.

It came as no surprise to locals when three members of gang (John and Simeon Reno and Franklin Sparks) launched a new innovation in thievery: train robbery. On October 6, 1866, the trio jumped on the Ohio & Mississippi train while it pulled out of the Seymour station, knocked out a guard, and tossed two safes from the moving boxcar a half mile east of the depot (100 feet east of the Burkart Blvd. railroad overpass). It was the nation's first train robbery. The Reno Gang got more than $10,000 from the Adams Express courier.

Emboldened by their success, they hit another train on September 28, 1867, and another on May 22, 1868, about 14 miles south of town by the Marshfield station, netting another $96,000 from Adams Express. Up to four Reno brothers, along with other Hoosier lowlifes, participated in these heists.

But you can only abuse a populace so long. A posse calling themselves the Seymour Regulators eventually caught up with several gang members on July 20, 1868. Val Elliott, Charles Roseberry, and Fred Clifton were pulled from a train and hanged from a tree beside the tracks near where Second St. crosses the B&O tracks today. On July 24, another three gang members—Frank Sparks, John Moore, and Henry Jerrell—were swinging from the same tree. Though the tree is long gone, locals still affectionately call the intersection "Hangman's Crossing."

Later that year, Frank Reno, William Reno, Simeon Reno, and Charles Anderson were yanked from their New Albany jail cells by an angry mob on December 12, 1868. The vigilantes didn't bother taking the brothers back to their favorite hanging tree, but lynched the robbers on the spot. The Regulators were not much for ceremony, so the three brothers were dumped in a common pine box and buried in Seymour. Years later, individual tombstones were erected over their grave.

Reno Brothers Grave, Old Seymour City Cemetery, 9th & Ewing, Seymour, IN 47274

No phone

Hours: Always visible

Cost: Free

Directions: Inside the iron fence just north of 9th St., halfway down the block west of Rte. 11.

SEYMOUR
Fish rained down in Seymour on August 8, 1891.

John Cougar Mellencamp was born in Seymour on October 7, 1951.

SHOALS
The team name at Shoals High School is the Jug Rox, named for a 60-foot, jug-shaped rock formation northwest of town.

SOLSBERRY
The Greene County Viaduct, five miles west of Solsberry off County Road 480E, is the second longest railroad trestle in the world, and the longest in the United States. It stands 180 feet high and is 2,295 feet long.

SULLIVAN
A Sullivan coal mine explosion on February 20, 1925, killed 52.

Spencer
Big Chicken

Standing atop a large pole at the southern entrance to the Owen County Fairgrounds is one of the largest chickens you'll ever see. No, it isn't the byproduct of selective breeding, nor a genetically engineered Franken-chicken, but a fiberglass statue that once stood outside a local restaurant. When the eatery went out of business, this mother of a clucker was put to use guarding Spencer's agricultural showcase on the south side of town.

Owen County Fairgrounds, Clay & Cooper Sts., Spencer, IN 47460

No phone

Hours: Always visible

Cost: Free

Directions: Turn south on East St., two blocks west of the Rte. 23 intersection; East turns to Clay at the railroad tracks, follow Clay to the fairgrounds.

Top rock head in Stone Head.

Stone Head
Stone Head

You don't have to have a stone head to live in Stone Head, but it helps. In fact, little is left of this community but the Stone Head after which it was named. The roadside bust was carved in 1851 by Henry Cross as part of his obligation to the local govern-ment. At the time, able-bodied men were required to put in several days labor on public works projects around Brown County in addition to paying taxes. Cross proposed to work off his six-days-a-year obligation by carving three busts to place on roadside markers along New Bellsville Pike, and since one was going to be of the venerable George Summa, the road's supervisor, officials agreed.

Two of the busts on the old road are long gone, and one remains: the Stone Head of Stone Head. Today it is painted white with black features, the stern face of a humorless mime. It has seen happier times, and so has the town of Stone Head.

Route 135, Stone Head, IN 47448
No phone
Hours: Always visible
Cost: Free
Directions: South of Rte. 46 on Rte. 135.

Tell City and Cannelton
Finding Out the Hard Way

As originally designed, the Lockheed Electra turbojet had one major flaw, but nobody realized it until St. Patrick's Day in 1960. Northwest Airlines Flight 710 was flying from Minneapolis to Miami when engine vibration caused another, sympathetic vibration in its wings, causing both to snap off at 18,000 feet. Without wings, the fuselage rocketed toward the earth, plowing into a soybean field at 600 MPH. All 63 aboard perished in the plane, which literally buried itself on impact.

Only eight of the victims were identified. The remains of the 55 others were interred in 16 coffins in a Tell City cemetery beneath a monument donated by Northwest Airlines. The Cannelton Kiwanis Club erected a similar monument at the crash site along the Ohio River.

Crash Memorial, Millstone Rd. (County Rd. 4), Cannelton, IN 47520
No phone
Hours: Always visible
Cost: Free
Directions: Southeast from Cannelton on Rte. 66, turn south on Rte. 166 to Millstone
  Rd., follow the signs east one mile, on the north side of the road.

Victims Graves, Greenwood Cemetery, Cemetery Rd. & Payne St. (Rte. 37), Tell City, IN 47586
(812) 547-6872
Hours: Always visible
Cost: Free
Directions: On Rte. 37, east of the Rte. 66 intersection.

TELL CITY

A statue of **William Tell** and his trusting son Walther stands in front of City Hall in Tell City. Swiss settlers colonized the area in 1856 under the guidance of Casper Gloor.

Wacky shack.

Vandalia
The Barn House

What is the Barn House? Imagine a 41-room wacky shack built from the remnants of 11 barns and 7 homes, with 74 roof angles and two ramshackle towers jutting 70 feet into the sky. It's as if Dr. Seuss contracted an over-caffeinated hillbilly to erect a dream home on a $37 budget.

According to the building's creator, Jim Pendleton, no two adjoining rooms are perpendicular to one another. Because there are so many walls, staircases, ladders, and windows, you must take him at his word. The joint is filled with dumpster-dive sofas, disconnected appliances, and refuse from 30 years of squatting hippies, beer-guzzling teens, and traveling lookie-loos.

Best of all, the Barn House is open to the public, or at least those who've read and acknowledged the "Enter at Your Own Risk" signs posted around the property. For all its slapped-together appearance, the 7,240-square-foot structure feels remarkably sturdy . . . even at the top of each tower. Pendleton began the project in 1972, but it took about 10 years to get it *just* right.

Bixler Road, Vandalia, IN 47460

Private phone

Hours: Daylight

Cost: Donations encouraged

Directions: Four miles west of Vandalia on Rte. 46, turn south on Bixler Rd.

Vevay
Mary Wright's Creepy Piano

Mary Wright was a creepy woman. She was the child of English immigrants who came to the new frontier in 1817 with a pile of money and a Muzio Clementi piano, the first ever seen in the yet-to-be state of Indiana. Before long, they had nothing left but the piano, and no way to return to their homeland. Mary did not take this well, for her true love was back in London. In her depression, she hid away on the second floor of her parents' home, coming downstairs once a week, in full dress, to give a morose recital for anyone who would listen . . . not that she cared if anyone showed up. This Emily Dickinson wannabe never acknowledged those who'd come to hear her play, and she performed until her death.

Today, Wright's Muzio Clementi is part of the collection of the Switzerland County Historical Museum. If you visit, don't miss the second floor, where you'll see Vevay's retired Electrostatic Shock Machine. A certain "Mr. Henry" used this device for many years at the local high school for "rejuvenating." Perhaps Mary could have benefited from a few volts.

Switzerland County Historical Museum, Market & Main Sts., Vevay, IN 47043

(812) 427-3560

Hours: April–October, Wednesday–Sunday 12:30–4:30 P.M.

Cost: Adults $1

www.switzcpl.lib.in.us/historicalsociety.html

Directions: Two blocks north on Rte. 156 from the Rte. 56 intersection.

TREVLAC

The town of Trevlac was named by founder Colonel Calvert, who simply spelled Calvert backward.

VEVAY

The preserved Switzerland County courthouse in Vevay has its original six-sided privy.

VINCENNES

Territorial governor and future President **William Henry Harrison** built a home dubbed Grouseland [3 W. Scott St., (812) 882-2096] in Vincennes in 1803–04. It was the first brick building constructed in Indiana; his family lived there until 1812.

"Big Sam," a 12-foot rattlesnake, terrorized Vincennes residents along the Little Wabash River from 1881 to 1908. It was eventually shot by farmer O. H. Sullivan.

Comedian **Red (Richard) Skelton** was born at 111 W. Lyndale Ave. in Vincennes on July 18, 1913, and lived there until he joined the circus at the age of 12.

Vincennes
Trigger-Happy Warship

There have been four ships in the U.S. Navy christened the USS *Vincennes*. The first three were low-tech: a 24-gun sloop (1826–1865); CA-44, a heavy cruiser (1937–1942), and CL-64, a light cruiser (1944–1946). But the last ship, CG-49, an Aegis Cruiser launched in 1985, was a sight to behold. Outfitted with every modern weapon system under the sun, this ship bragged that it could shoot down incoming planes before they ever became a threat.

And it did. On July 3, 1988, it fired on what it thought was an enemy fighter plane in the Persian Gulf and turned out to be an Iranian airliner with 290 innocent civilians aboard. Trying to explain the disastrous incident as a reasonable boo-boo, the Navy initially claimed the plane was traveling outside a commercial air lane (it wasn't), that it made suspicious maneuvers (it hadn't), that it didn't appear on the radar as a commercial flight (it did), or that perhaps it was being shadowed by an Iranian fighter (not true). An extensive investigation revealed the cause of the accident was a crew whose technological firepower far exceeded their personal limitations. Under stress, they saw the radar blip as an enemy aircraft because they expected it to be.

A monument to this vessel, and the three other ships bearing this town's name, stands north of the George Rogers Clark Memorial in Vincennes.

Lincoln Memorial Bridge, First & W. Vigo Sts., Vincennes, IN 47591

(800) 886-6443 or (812) 886-0400

Hours: Always visible

Cost: Free

www.foxcomm.net/web2/dilbert/vincennes.html

Directions: Business Rte. 50 at the Wabash River.

YELLOWWOOD STATE FOREST

A 500-pound boulder was found wedged in the crook of a tree 35 feet above the ground in the Yellowwood State Forest near "Gobbler Rock." Nobody has been able to explain how it got there.

How the other half lived.
Photo by author, courtesy of Historic Landmark Foundation of Indiana

West Baden Springs
The New West Baden Springs Hotel

Back when Las Vegas was a few shacks more than a desert, French Lick and West Baden Springs were vacation destinations for the rich and famous. In 1902, the West Baden Springs Hotel set a new standard for elegance and over-the-top architecture. Its central dome had a 200-foot diameter, larger than St. Peter's Basilica in Rome, and was the largest unsupported dome in the world until the Louisiana Superdome was built in New Orleans. On the grounds, the resort had a double-decker riding track—the top floor for bicyclists and the bottom for horse-drawn carriages—circling around a baseball diamond. Visitors such as Helen Keller, Al Capone, and Gen. John J. Pershing could stroll through the elaborate gardens, relax in the Roman baths, or drink the spring's "Sprudel Water" that was said to cure almost anything.

With the stock market collapse of 1929, the hotel closed its doors and started its downhill slide. At one time it was used as the winter home of the Hagenbeck-Wallace Circus. Then, in 1934, it was sold to the Jesuits for $1. They proceeded to tear out anything too costly to repair, which was a lot. From 1966 to 1983, it was home to the Northwoods Institute, a private college. As it fell further into disrepair, it was rescued by the Historic Landmark Foundation of Indiana and given a $34 million restoration (most of it from the Cook Group), about half of what is needed to complete the job. The National Historic Landmark is now open to any buyer who will finish the work. Today, West Baden Springs is open for tours, and well worth the $10 admission.

Contact: Historic Landmarks Foundation of Indiana, 340 W. Michigan St., Indianapolis, IN 46202

(800) 450-4534 or (812) 936-4034

Hours: April–December, Monday–Saturday 10 A.M.–3 P.M., Sunday noon–4 P.M., tours on the hour; January–March, Wednesday–Sunday 11 A.M., 1 P.M., and 2 P.M. tours only

Cost: Adults $10

www.historiclandmarks.org

Directions: Due west of the railroad stop on Rte. 56.

ZOAR

The town of Zoar celebrates Mosquito Fest each August. Call (812) 536-2920 for information.

Worthington
Remnants of the World's Largest Deciduous Tree

Just try and take their branch, you Kokomoans!

Look out, Kokomo! Sure, that town might lay claim to the World's Largest Stump, but proud Worthingtonians are quick to point out that just because you have the largest *stump*, that doesn't mean you have the largest *tree*. In fact, the 150-foot-high sycamore that once grew a mile and a half west of town had, at its peak, a circumference of 45'3" at a foot above the ground. Its largest branch was 27'8" around, and another measured 23'3".

As powerful as it was, the tree toppled during a violent windstorm in 1925. Both the stump and largest branch were too large to save or move, so a smaller branch was transported to a local park. A roof was built to protect the blunt end from rain and snow, and the town bought a piece of surplus army artillery to guard it from jealous Kokomoans.

If you wonder whether the Pacific Northwest's redwoods dwarf this stupendous sycamore, you are engaging in technical hairsplitting, which proud Worthingtonians will not entertain. They said *deciduous*, and redwoods are *evergreens*.

City Park, Dayton & Worthington Sts., Worthington, IN 47471

No phone

Hours: Always visible

Cost: Free

Directions: Dayton St. runs parallel to Rte. 157, north–south, three blocks to the west; follow it to the north end of town to City Park.

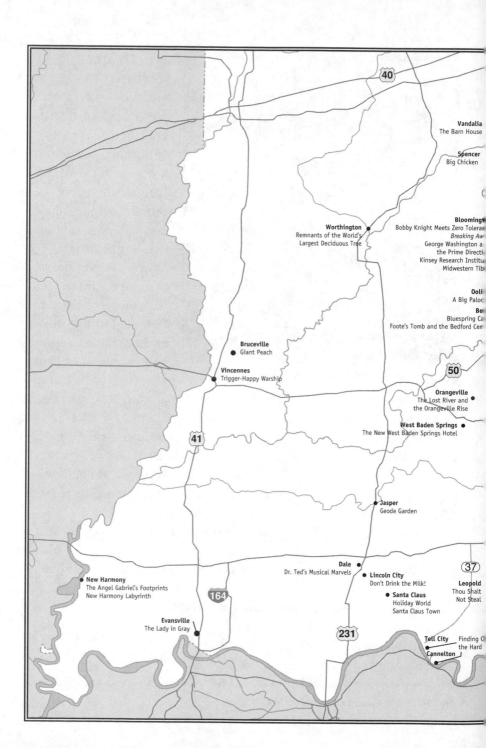

Vandalia
The Barn House

Spencer
Big Chicken

Bloomingt
Bobby Knight Meets Zero Tolera
Breaking Aw
George Washington a
the Prime Directi
Kinsey Research Institu
Midwestern Tib

Ooli
A Big Paloc

Be
Bluespring Ca
Foote's Tomb and the Bedford Cen

Bruceville
Giant Peach

Vincennes
Trigger-Happy Warship

Orangeville
The Lost River and
the Orangeville Rise

West Baden Springs
The New West Baden Springs Hotel

Jasper
Geode Garden

Dale
Dr. Ted's Musical Marvels

Lincoln City
Don't Drink the Milk!

Leopold
Thou Shalt
Not Steal

New Harmony
The Angel Gabriel's Footprints
New Harmony Labyrinth

Santa Claus
Holiday World
Santa Claus Town

Evansville
The Lady in Gray

Tell City   Finding O
the Hard
Cannelton

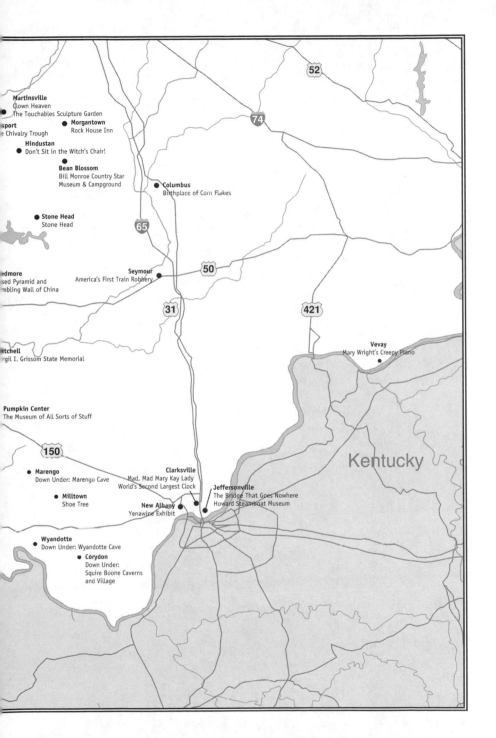

Martinsville
Clown Heaven
The Touchables Sculpture Garden

sport
e Chivalry Trough

Morgantown
Rock House Inn

Hindustan
Don't Sit in the Witch's Chair!

Bean Blossom
Bill Monroe Country Star
Museum & Campground

Columbus
Birthplace of Corn Flakes

Stone Head
Stone Head

dmore
sed Pyramid and
mbling Wall of China

Seymour
America's First Train Robbery

tchell
rgil I. Grissom State Memorial

Vevay
Mary Wright's Creepy Piano

Pumpkin Center
The Museum of All Sorts of Stuff

Kentucky

Marengo
Down Under: Marengo Cave

Clarksville
Mad, Mad Mary Kay Lady
World's Second Largest Clock

Jeffersonville
The Bridge That Goes Nowhere
Howard Steamboat Museum

Milltown
Shoe Tree

New Albany
Yenawine Exhibit

Wyandotte
Down Under: Wyandotte Cave

Corydon
Down Under:
Squire Boone Caverns
and Village

4

INDiaNaPOLiS Area

*I*ndianapolis sometimes has an undeserved reputation as being a Nowheresville, dismissed as Indiana-no-place. It is everything but. They've got the world's largest children's museum, sports and recreation facilities that rival most big cities, art, theater, fine dining, and more.

Yeah, yeah, yeah. Go read about that stuff somewhere else. You didn't purchase this guide looking for *culture*. You want to know about Elvis and David Letterman. You wonder what Jim Jones was doing selling South American monkeys door-to-door to residents of this fair city. And what happened to the local folks who tossed a former American president into a mud puddle? All good questions, and you'll soon have answers.

But first, let's talk about the birthplace of Wonder Bread . . .

Bread doesn't get much whiter than this.

Indianapolis
Birthplace of Wonder Bread

Don't act so surprised! If Wonder Bread hadn't been invented in Indianapolis, where do you think it might have been? This shockingly white bread was developed at the Taggart Baking Company in 1921. Vice-president Elmer Cline came up with the bread's name after seeing a balloon race at the Indianapolis Speedway; he claimed to be "filled with wonder," much the same way Wonder Bread seems to be filled with air. Taggart was sold to the Continental Baking Company in 1925, and they've been baking the loaves ever since.

If you're one of those folks who don't quite understand how every loaf of Wonder Bread can look *exactly* the same, who believe that their uniformity is achieved through some sort of nefarious process, you're invited along on the tour. The secret? "It's Slo-Baked." The backstage peek also divulges how Twinkies and Ding Dongs are manufactured.

Wonder and Hostess Bakery, 2929 N. Shadeland Ave., Indianapolis, IN 46219

(317) 547-9421

Hours: Call ahead for tour hours

Cost: Free

www.wonderbread.com

Directions: South of E. 30th St. on Shadeland Ave.

Daniel Boone, Tree Vandal

Though the truth of its origin is questionable at best, a marking on a tree in Indianapolis is attributed to Daniel Boone, who was a surveyor in the Northwest Territory around 1800. The carving on the beech's trunk gives Boone's name and trademark bear paw insignia. Some historians believe its location, high up on the trunk, was probably the result of Boone being on horseback when he carved it. Visitors to Eagle Creek are strongly discouraged from adding their own Boone-like insignias anywhere else in this park.

Eagle Creek Park, 7840 W. 56th St., Indianapolis, IN 46254

(317) 327-7148

E-mail: comments@eaglecreekpark-fdn.org

Hours: Daily 9 A.M.–dusk

Cost: Monday–Friday $2/car, Saturday–Sunday $3/car

www.eaglecreekpark-fdn.org/default.htm

Directions: Just west of I-465 on 56th St.; Boone Tree approximately one block north of the Nature Center.

INDIANAPOLIS

Mrs. Gilbert Van Camp invented tinned pork and beans in Indianapolis in the late 1800s.

David Letterman, Bag Boy

David Letterman was born in Indianapolis on April 12, 1947. His family lived in the Broad Ripple neighborhood, and his father owned the first FTD florist shop in the city. Dave attended Public School 55 (now Eliza A. Blaker Elementary, 1349 E. 54th St.) and seemed to be living the life of typical Baby Boomer . . . until he got a job as a bag boy.

Why the Atlas Supermarket was so instrumental in Letterman's comic development is no mystery; kindhearted owner Sidney Maurer not only tolerated Letterman's pranks, but would cover for the teenager when customers failed to appreciate the humor. Other bosses might have fired the smartass. Letterman held raffles for sports cars that didn't exist. More than once he announced that a mah-jongg tournament would be held on Sunday and players would show up with their tiles to find an empty parking lot and a locked store. Other times he conducted fire drills and marched confused customers out into the parking lot.

Letterman attended Broad Ripple High School (1115 Broad Ripple Ave.), where he served as a hall monitor, from 1961 to 1965. Marilyn Quayle also attended Broad Ripple, but was two years younger than Dave (and remembered not liking him very much).

After college and a short stint at a radio station in Muncie, Dave returned to Indy in 1970 with his wife Michelle, where he held a five-year "temporary" job at WLWI-TV (Channel 13, now WTHR). His first job was to read the station's call letters and public service announcements, but he was later given a few shows. He hosted the 2 A.M. *Freeze-Dried Movie*, a Saturday morning 4-H show called *Clover Power*, and the weekend weather. As a meteorologist, he took liberties with the forecasts, making up tropical storms and town names, and pissed off local farmers in the process. In 1975, he left for California to become a stand-up comedian.

Atlas Supermarket, 5411 N. College, Indianapolis, IN 46220

(317) 255-6800

Hours: Monday–Saturday 9 A.M.–7 P.M.

Cost: Free

Directions: Seven blocks east of Meridian (Rte. 31) at 54th St.

Elvis's Last Concert

When Elvis Presley played Market Square Arena on June 26, 1977, his career was fading fast. The 45-minute concert before a pitiful turnout of 18,000 would go down in history as the low point before his last big comeback . . . after dying six weeks later. The King stayed at the Stouffer's Hotel on War Memorial Square, and didn't even have the energy to shoot out the TV.

By dying early in his Graceland bathroom, Elvis unknowingly transformed himself from a has-been rocker to a forever-will-be legend. A local fan club gathers every year on the anniversary of his final act to remember their idol and console one another. When Market Square Arena was demolished a few years ago, the commemorative plaque was moved to the new Conseco Fieldhouse (www.consecofieldhouse.com) a few blocks away and mounted on the south side of the building. But you can't pull a fast one on Elvis fans—they know where their idol tossed his last sweaty scarf!

Market Square Arena, 330 E. Market St., Indianapolis, IN 46204

No phone

Hours: Original site torn down; plaque moved to the Conseco Fieldhouse

Cost: Free

Directions: Between Alabama and New Jersey, east of the Indiana War Memorial.

INDIANAPOLIS

TV's *One Day at a Time* was set in Indianapolis.

President **Benjamin Harrison** lived at 1230 N. Delaware St. in Indianapolis from 1875 until his death, leaving only to serve one term in the White House from 1889 to 1893. Harrison died here on March 13, 1901, of pneumonia. Call (317) 631-1898 for a tour.

On May 16, 1984, garbage fell from the sky over Indianapolis: plastic cups, paper, computer printouts. The trash was traced to a dump several miles away, but nobody could explain how it dropped from above without any storms in the area.

Hannah House

According to legend, a basement fire ignited by an overturned lamp in this 1858 mansion killed several former slaves, and, rather than having this station on the Underground Railroad exposed, the runaways' bodies were buried secretly beneath the house. Things haven't been the same since.

Moaning, phantom footsteps, and mysterious scratching noises are par for the course. There's also the smell of rotting flesh in the upstairs bedrooms, but that could just be a dead rat in the walls. Some have seen the ghost of a stillborn baby; far from being still, it tends to run around the second floor. And when *P.M. Magazine* was filming a segment on the hauntings, a chandelier swung unassisted and a picture leapt from its nail on the wall.

3801 Madison Ave., Indianapolis, IN 46225

(317) 955-0741

Hours: Call ahead

Cost: Free

Directions: At the southeast corner of National and Madison Aves.

Indiana Medical History Museum

The Indiana Medical History Museum is one of the hidden gems of Indianapolis, tucked away on the grounds of the old Central State Hospital for the Insane. It is housed in the nation's oldest pathology building, built in 1898 under the direction of Dr. George Edenharter. The facility had three cutting-edge laboratories, a library, a photography studio, an anatomical museum, a morgue, and an amphitheater used for its teaching program. Edenharter's facility was a leader in the study of syphilis (particularly as it affected the brain), mental illness, and brain injuries.

The current museum has over 15,000 artifacts in its collection, but remarkably few of them are out on display. Instead, the building has been restored to the way it looked shortly after it was opened to give visitors a sense of what it might have looked like a century ago. In one room on the ground floor, jars filled with brains and parts of brains fill cabinets along two walls. The curators admit this is the room school kids enjoy the most.

Old Pathology Building, 3045 W. Vermont St., Indianapolis, IN 46222

(317) 635-7329

E-mail: Edenharter@aol.com

Hours: Thursday–Saturday 10 A.M.–3:30 P.M.

Cost: Adults $5, Kids (K–12) $1

www.imhm.org

Directions: Two blocks south of Michigan St., three blocks west of N. Warren Ave.

Popcorn landmark.

Indiana Walk of Legends

Laugh if you will, but Hoosiers are proud of their progeny: Orville Redenbacher, John Cougar Mellencamp, Eli Lilly, Earl Butz . . . they're all here on the Indiana Walk of Legends! Sadly, most are commemorated with signatures in cement without footprints à la Grauman's, so you can't see if your shoes match those of the Popcorn King.

The best time to view the Walk of Legends is the off-season, since it's free to enter the state fairgrounds when the fair isn't in progress. You also won't have to fight the throngs of Earl Butz groupies who come each year.

Indiana State Fairgrounds, 1202 E. 38th St., Indianapolis, IN 46205

(317) 927-7500

Hours: Always visible

Cost: Free

www.state.in.us/statefair/

Directions: Enter from Parkway Dr. (Rte. 37) entrance, drive forward past the Coliseum, turn right at the end of the lot, in front of the buildings at the northwest corner.

King Tut and the Scots

Two Indianapolis buildings look distinctly out of place in this Midwestern city, and both were built by Masons: the Murat Temple and the Scottish Rite Cathedral. And if you think these so-called "secret societies" are mysterious, you haven't visited with the chatty guides at the Scottish Rite Cathedral. Just try to escape without fistfuls of literature about their organization.

As you'll learn on the tour, the gothic cathedral was built from 1927 to 1929 using the number 33 (the number of degrees in the Masonic Rite) as a reference. There are 33 windows, 33 feet between pillars, 33 foot-square tiles between pillars, and so on. You'll see all the main rooms in the elaborate structure, including the grand hall where the elaborately costumed induction ceremonies are performed. Believe it or not, a new member can move through 32 rites on two successive Saturdays, and they are no more painful than two evenings at Siegfried and Roy.

Ancient Accepted Scottish Rite, 650 N. Meridian St., Indianapolis, IN 46204

(800) 489-3579

Hours: Tours, Saturday 9 A.M.–2:30 P.M.

Cost: Free

www.aasr-indy.org

Directions: Four blocks west of the Murat Temple at Meridian St. (Rte. 31).

If you obtain the Masons' 33rd Rite, you become a Shriner and move down the street to the Murat Temple, headquarters of the Mystic Shrine. This Middle Eastern–style structure was built in 1910 and contains one of the largest theaters in town. The interior is designed with a King Tut motif, complete with murals, tile work, and stained glass. Their lounge is open to non-Shriners for lunch.

The Shriners are much more formal than the Scots, wear fezzes, and drive around in tiny cars. They also raise an incredible amount of money for children's hospitals and volunteer as clowns, which makes it easy to forgive them for the silly, pseudomystical antics.

Murat Temple (Oasis of Indianapolis, Desert of Indiana), 510 N. New Jersey St., Indianapolis, IN 46204

(800) 535-7270 or (317) 635-2433

E-mail: gjh@in-motion.net

Lounge Hours: Monday–Friday 11 A.M.–2 P.M.

Cost: Free

www.muratshrine.org

Directions: At the intersection of Massachusetts Ave. and New Jersey St.

Mega-Popcorn Blast

It is more than a little bizarre that only steps from the Indiana Walk of Fame's tribute to Orville Redenbacher is the site of the world's most deadly popcorn-related tragedy. It happened on Halloween night in 1963. Thousands were watching a "Holiday on Ice" show at the State Fairground Arena, unaware of a liquid propane gas leak beneath the grandstands. The gas was used to fuel an industrial popcorn popper in a concession stand and had been accumulating for hours. Finally, a spark from an improperly wired machine ignited the flammable gas. The explosion blew a section of the first-class seats onto the rink and into the cheaper folding chairs on the opposite side of the arena. In all, 73 were killed and 340 more were injured.

Oddly enough, this wasn't the first time that a crowd perished at the state fairgrounds due to an explosion. On October 1, 1869, the blast from an overheated boiler caused a stampede that left 27 dead fairgoers in its wake.

Pepsi Coliseum, Indiana State Fairgrounds, 1202 E. 38th St., Indianapolis, IN 46205

(317) 927-7500

Hours: Always visible

Cost: Free

www.state.in.us/statefair/rentals/buildings/coliseum.html

Directions: Enter from Parkway Drive (Rte. 37) entrance; the Coliseum is ahead on the left.

INDIANAPOLIS

Author **Kurt Vonnegut** was born in Indianapolis on November 11, 1922. He attended Shortridge High School, graduating in 1940.

Mike Tyson Gets into Trouble

In retrospect, perhaps it wasn't a great idea to have Mike Tyson judge the Miss Black America Pageant at the 1991 Black Expo in Indianapolis. Before and during the show he was said to have taken a hands-on approach to the contestants; 11 of the 23 contestants filed a joint $21 million lawsuit against what they labeled a "serial buttocks fondler."

But his groping troubles didn't even compare with the mistakes he made by inviting Miss Rhode Island, Desiree Washington, up to his hotel room at 2 A.M. on July 19, 1991. Exactly what happened in Suite 606 became cause for debate. Tyson claimed Washington wanted revenge after they had consensual sex and he told her "The limousine is downstairs. If you don't want to use the limousine, you can walk." Washington claimed Tyson raped her.

The jury believed Washington's account, and Tyson was convicted on one count of rape and two counts of criminal deviant sexual behavior. He was sentenced to six years at the Indiana Youth Center in Plainfield (727 Moon Rd.), and he served about three years. While there, he claimed to have read a lot: "When I was in prison, I was wrapped up in all those deep books. That Tolstoy crap. People shouldn't read that stuff."

Canterbury Hotel, Suite 606, 123 S. Illinois, Indianapolis, IN 46225

(800) 538-8186 or (317) 634-3000

E-mail: info@canterburyhotel.com

Hours: Always visible

Cost: Free

www.canterburyhotel.com

Directions: One block west of Meridian St. (Rte. 37), two blocks south of Washington St.

INDIANAPOLIS

Dr. Richard Gatling invented the machine gun in Indianapolis in 1862. The first model shot 250 rounds per minute, but soon got up to 500. His stated goal, after witnessing the Civil War, was to invent a weapon so horrible that nobody would dare use it. Nice theory.

It is illegal to send flowers to anyone incarcerated in an Indianapolis jail.

Go ahead—take a sip!

The Original People's Temple

Jim Jones and his wife Marceline made a big impression on Indianapolis during the 1950s and '60s. Arriving in the summer of 1951, the couple brought along their pet chimpanzee, very little money, and a burning desire to minister to (and some say fleece) the poor. Jones started as a student pastor at the south side's Somerset Methodist Church but didn't enjoy playing second or third fiddle to anyone.

Jones left Somerset to start his own ministry, Community Unity, and lived in a bungalow on nearby Villa Street. To raise funds to fix the place up, he sold South American monkeys door-to-door at $29 a pop, grossing $50,000. That's over 1,700 monkeys! He was also invited to be a guest minister at the nearby Laurel Street Tabernacle, where he became well known for healings that included yanking cancerous blobs from (supposedly) sick parishioners. Marceline helped with the act.

Laurel Street never brought Jones on full-time, mostly because he was actively recruiting African Americans, so in 1956 Jones headed to the north side to found a new, larger church. He christened it "Wings of

Deliverance," a name he soon changed to "The People's Temple." His message attracted many poor and liberal followers. He opened food and clothing banks, created soup kitchens, took poor kids to the zoo, and delivered free coal to shut-ins. He also helped to integrate at least one Indianapolis hospital. The message was so successful that, a year later, Jim and Marceline moved the congregation to a former synagogue at 10th St. and Delaware (destroyed by fire in 1975), and their home to a duplex at 2327 N. Broadway.

But Jim had his dark side. When he felt his congregation wasn't attentive enough, he threw his Bible on the ground, spit on it, and announced, "Too many people are looking at this and not ME!" He devised an elaborate scheme where People's Temple members ran local businesses that channeled money back into the church, a plan that would eventually force him to move westward.

In 1961, the governor appointed Jones director of the Indianapolis Human Rights Commission. He used the position to draw more attention to himself, but some of the attention came from tax investigators and creditors. Paranoid (and rightly so) that he would soon be found out, he announced in 1965 that the congregation would move to Ukiah, California, to escape an upcoming holocaust unleashed by the Bomb. According to an article he'd read, Ukiah was naturally protected from radioactive fallout. Jones led a westward-bound caravan of 100 or so faithful with his black Cadillac. He held a $100,000 check, but still owed Indiana creditors $40,000.

House of Deliverance (former home of Community Unity; not affiliated), 720 S. Randolph, Indianapolis, IN 46203

(317) 916-5838

Hours: Sevices, Tuesday 7 P.M., Thursday 7 P.M., Sunday 9:30 A.M., 6 P.M.

Cost: Free

Directions: Six blocks west of S. Keystone Ave., three blocks north to Hoyt Ave.

Abundant Faith Apostolic Church (former home of People's Temple; not affiliated), 1502 N. New Jersey, Indianapolis, IN 46202

(317) 972-9474

Hours: Services, Sunday Noon, Wednesday 7 P.M., Monday 7 P.M.

Cost: Free

Directions Five blocks east of Meridian (Rte. 37), one block south of 16th St.

Sleep in a Train

If you want to sleep in a train as riders used to, you have two options: sneak into a railyard and find an open boxcar, or head to Indianapolis and the Crowne Plaza Hotel. The first is inexpensive, but you run the risk of having your skull split open by a railyard goon. There's no danger of that at the Crowne Plaza. Parked within the city's old Union Station train shed, 26 nonmoving Pullman cars have been converted into Victorian guest rooms. These cars are sealed off from the rest of the hotel, so the only way to see them up close is to book one for the night.

If you only want to stroll through, the Crowne Plaza's lobby and hall-ways are filled with creepy white statues of passengers frozen in time, forever waiting for a train that never arrives. Kind of like Amtrak.

Crowne Plaza Union Station, 123 W. Louisiana St., Indianapolis, IN 46225

(800) 2-CROWNE (227-6963)

E-mail: indycrowne@genhotels.com

Hours: Always open

Cost: $165–$200

indycrowne@ameritech.net

Directions: Just west of Meridian St., four blocks south of Monument Circle.

INDIANAPOLIS

Actor **Clifton Webb** was born Webb Parmelee Hollenbeck in Indianapolis on November 19, 1891.

Indiana poet **James Whitcomb Riley** lived at 528 Lockerbie St. in Indianapolis from 1893 until his death on July 22, 1916. For a tour of the home, call (317) 631-5885.

A four-foot alligator was caught by fisherman Jack Herring in the White River near Indianapolis on August 14, 1999.

Jane Pauley was born in Indianapolis on October 31, 1950. She attended Warren Central High School (9500 E. 16th St.), graduating in 1968, and was a member of the Prom Court.

No longer lost at sea.

USS Indianapolis Memorial

In the final days of World War II, the USS *Indianapolis* delivered a shipment of uranium to Tinian Island in the Pacific. This material would later be used for the bombs dropped on Hiroshima and Nagasaki. The heavy cruiser was headed home when it was torpedoed by a Japanese submarine on the night of July 29–30, 1945. The ship sank quickly and, due to poor radio communications, no one knew the ship had gone down or even that it was overdue. Consequently, no rescue party was launched.

Of the *Indianapolis*'s crew of 1,197, about 900 made it into the water that night, but only 317 were pulled alive from the water five days later. The survivors were saved only by a chance sighting of their oil slick by a passing aircraft. Most died of injuries or dehydration, but many were eaten by sharks. Quint (Robert Shaw) would recount the story in the movie *Jaws*.

Captain Charles Butler McVay III was court-martialed for failing to zigzag his ship to avoid being torpedoed, though the Navy had clearly told him he would encounter no submarines on his journey (a fact they knew to be untrue). McVay was the only commander of the 700 vessels sunk in the war to be court-martialed. Blamed by victim's families in a constant stream of hate letters, McVay committed suicide in 1968.

In 1996, an 11-year-old boy named Hunter Scott began asking questions after seeing *Jaws*. Surprisingly, he uncovered new evidence pointing to culpability by Navy brass, errors that had led to the ship's sinking. This information led to a Congressional inquiry, which posthumously cleared McVay. A recent monument to all the crew now stands in Indianapolis, the city that gave the ship its name.

Ellsworth & Walnut Sts., Indianapolis, IN 46202

No phone

Hours: Always visible

Cost: Free

www.ussindianapolis.org/resolution.htm

Directions: Five blocks south of 10th St., take Walnut St. west seven blocks to Ellsworth St.

Paul Bunyon's gardening tool.

World's Largest Trowel

Have you ever had one of those ambitious gardening weekends where, by the time the sun went down on Sunday, only about half of your annuals were in the ground? Well, perhaps you weren't using the right tool. If you used one of those kitchen-spoon-sized trowels, perhaps that was your problem. You needed something a bit more industrial—like the trowel at Habig's Gardening Center.

This T-rex trowel could dig out your entire flower bed with one scoop. Properly mounted on the front of a small tractor, it could also be used by undertakers to plant dead gardeners who want to return to the earth, compost style.

Habig's Gardening Center, 5201 N. College, Indianapolis, IN 46205

(317) 283-5412

Hours: Always visible

Cost: Free

Directions: Eight blocks east of Meridian St. (Rte. 31) at 52nd St.

Here's Dad Jones.

Suburbs
Avon
Dead Dad Jones

Dad Jones was a worker on the Inter-Urban Railroad project west of Indianapolis when he was tragically entombed in cement after the platform on which he was standing collapsed, plunging him into a concrete grave. The quick-drying cement below had been poured for a bridge piling. Rather than fish the poor guy out (and slow down the work), his body was left inside, where it remains to this day . . . or so the story goes.

After trains began running on the line, folks started noticing weird things. When a train crossed the trestle, some could hear the screams of Dad's ghost, trapped in the foundation, squished by the weight of the passenger cars. After the train passed, he would thump on the cement with his fists until he could pound no more. Other witnesses claim that water condenses on the piling and oozes red, like blood. While particularly visible on the night of a full moon, you can clearly see from this photo that something's seeping out in broad daylight.

Urban legend or OSHA violation? Stop by on a moonlit night and decide for yourself.

Lick Creek Bridge, Center St., Avon, IN 46123

No phone

Hours: Always visible

Cost: Free

Directions: Turn south off Rte. 40 on Center St., three blocks west of the Rte. 267 intersection.

INDIANAPOLIS

Three truck drivers on I-70 near Indianapolis were encircled with a lampshadelike ring of blue light on March 29, 1978. After the blue light went out, one trucker requested aloud to be taken with the "UFO" and the light popped on again for another 15 seconds.

Fifty-three people were killed in an Indianapolis train crash on October 31, 1903. Many of the dead were Purdue football players headed to play Indiana University. Their train rear-ended a couple of coal cars at a switch.

BEECH GROVE

Steve McQueen was born in Beech Grove on March 24, 1930.

FISHERS

Actress **Frances Farmer** is buried at Oak Lawn Memorial Gardens (9700 Allisonville Rd.) in Fishers.

Carmel

Illusions

Walk into this eatery in a north suburban strip mall, and you'll soon know something's up. The lobby is decorated to look like a silk plant forest. Look around and you'll find a sword stuck in a stone. Pull on the handle to get in . . . or be crowned king or queen of England! Is this some type of Arthurian eatery? Perhaps—nothing is quite as it seems at Illusions.

A host/hostess trained in prestidigitation leads you to your table. Where are the menus? Ta-dah! Here they are! Could we get another set of silverware? Presto! After ordering from the mystical menu, you'll be approached by roving magicians who will amaze you with card tricks and disappearing scarves. Feel free to tip, and if the act wasn't so good, suggest that they pull a quarter from your ear.

If you're really into magic come on a weekend, when they have performers in the adjoining Disappearing Nightly Showroom.

969 Keystone Way, Carmel, IN 46032

(317) 575-8312

Hours: Monday–Thursday 5–9 P.M., Friday 4:30–10 P.M., Saturday 4:30–10:30 P.M.;
   Disappearing Nightly shows, Friday–Saturday 9, 10, and 11 P.M.

Cost: Meals $8–$20

www.illusionsrestaurant.com

Directions: One block west of N. Keystone Ave. (Rte. 431) on E. Carmel Dr., just north of
   Merchants Square Mall.

Museum of Miniature Houses and Other Collections

Doll houses are more than just elaborate toys for little children, they're windows to the past, as you'll see at this small museum of even smaller buildings. An antique doll house might reflect decorating styles at the time they were built, as well as the sorts of objects found in a typical home, much the same way a pink Barbie Dreamhouse reflects our current ideal lifestyle.

OK, so maybe using doll houses for historical research is a bit of a stretch, but they're cool nonetheless. The oldest doll house in this museum's collection has a short message hidden beneath the wallpaper on a back wall by Thomas Russell in 1861, a father's message to his daughter. Other pieces in the collections could more accurately be called scenes, like a princess running through a forest blanketed in snow, past unicorns and trees draped in jewels, followed by her Prince Charming. Yikes—the girl who owned that one was in for a surprise.

111 E. Main St., Carmel, IN 46032

(317) 575-9466

E-mail: mmhaoc@aol.com

Hours: Wednesday–Saturday 11 A.M.–4 P.M., Sunday 1–4 P.M.

Cost: Adults $3, Kids (under 10) $1

www.museumofminiatures.org/index.htm

Directions: One block east of Rangeline Rd. on Main St. (131st St.).

World's First Traffic Light

Local electrician Leslie Haines had a great idea to help auto drivers avoid accidents in Carmel's main intersection—a stoplight! But his 1923 invention had one major flaw: it had no yellow. Without a warning that the lights would turn, motorists received an excessive number of tickets for running red lights. Long after it was clear that the well-intentioned device was inadequate, it was removed in 1934.

Today you'll find a standard, three-color stoplight at the intersection of Main Street and Rangeline Road. Haines's contraption is in the possession of the Carmel-Clay Historical Society where it can't hurt anyone.

Main St. & Rangeline Rd., Carmel, IN 46032

No phone

Hours: Always visible

Cost: Free

Directions: On 131st St. (Main St.) in the center of town.

Carmel-Clay Historical Society, 211 First St. SW, Carmel, IN 46032

(317) 846-7117

Hours: Friday 9 A.M.–5 P.M., Saturday 10 A.M.–4 P.M., Sunday 2–4 P.M.

Cost: Free

Directions: Two blocks west and one block south of the intersection.

ZIONSVILLE

Zionsville has one of the nation's three Rolls-Royce dealerships, Albers Rolls Royce (360 S. First St.). It is not open to the general public.

Hands-on democracy.

Plainfield
Dump the
President!

There was a time when the American public took a more active role in national politics. The case of the Van Buren Elm is a prime example.

As president, Martin Van Buren vetoed an appropriation bill for improvements to the National Road. This enraged voters along the essential east–west artery, an anger that didn't subside until 1842. Van Buren was then an ex-president, traveling through Plainfield by carriage. Locals had coached his driver to aim for a particularly large pothole along their still-unimproved road. The carriage tipped, and old Martin was dumped out into a mud puddle. For his successful effort, the driver received a silk hat. The tree at the site became known as the Van Buren Elm. And no other president blocked funding; the National Road was completed by 1851.

The original Van Buren Elm fell victim to Dutch elm disease, but it has been replaced by a new sapling—so watch out, all you present and future office holders!

Friends' Meetinghouse, 205 S. East St., Plainfield, IN 46168

No phone

Hours: Always visible

Cost: Free

Directions: One block west of the Rte. 267 intersection with Rte. 40 (East St.).

Speedway
The Speedway and Hall of Fame Museum

The Speedway and Hall of Fame Museum is both the state's most-visited attraction and one of the coolest. You don't have to be a rabid fan of the sport to get goose bumps as you drive onto the grounds through a tunnel beneath the grandstand and track—the museum is on the infield!

There are about 75 autos on display, from the first racers in 1911 to the most recent winners. You'll also see the fastest Indy winner (Arie Luyendyk's Lola-Chevy at 185.981 MPH average) and Eddie Ricken-backer's 1914 Duesenberg. The World War I flying ace owned the speed-way from 1927 to 1945, and is fondly remembered . . . er . . . perhaps not by the Germans. The cars are all in tip-top shape. Mangled racers in which drivers passed on to that great Brickyard-in-the-Sky are NOT on display. You'll learn plenty about the Memorial Day race, like how (reportedly) 70 percent of auto improvements have originated here, from the rearview mirror to balloon tires. One vehicle is available for photo ops, though think twice about whether you want to squeeze in for a pic-ture—this car isn't exactly roomy.

Don't pass on the Track Tour just to save the extra $3; it's the best part of the visit. Guides take you on one lap around the track in a rental-car shuttle van (after announcing "Gentlemen, start your engines!"). Along your journey, you'll hear interesting facts: the 2.5-mile track has curves that bank at 9°12' the track began as a testing facility in 1909; and most of the Brickyard's original 3 million bricks are still just below the concrete surface. You'll stop in front of the green pagoda-shaped viewing tower to take photos of the only brick still exposed, the finish line. In the time it takes you to putt around the track just once, a typical race car would have lapped you 15 or 16 times.

The Speedway, 4790 W. 16th St., Speedway, IN 46222

(317) 484-6747

Hours: June–April, daily 9 A.M.–5 P.M.; May till 6 P.M.

Cost: Adults $3, Kids (5–16) $1, Track Tour $3

www.brickyard.com

Directions: Crawfordsville Rd. Exit from I-465; head southeast until you reach 16th St.

5

DiLLiNGer'S
DiaPerS-to-DeatH Tour

John Dillinger was front page news in 1934—bold, fearless, and one hundred percent Hoosier. Though his deadly crime spree began in the summer of 1933, he wasn't a national superstar until he made daring escapes from jails in Lima, Ohio, and Crown Point, Indiana, and from FBI dragnets in St. Paul, Minnesota, and the Little Bohemia Lodge in Manitowish Waters, Wisconsin.

Dillinger seldom operated alone. He and his fellow thugs were known as the Terror Gang. The Indiana governor and National Guard proposed using tanks and poison gas to fight them. In retrospect it might have made the fight more balanced, for it was later learned the gang had once planned to raid the Fort Harrison arsenal for mortars and more powerful weapons.

The American Legion offered to deputize 30,000 of its members for roadblocks and posses. Though the plan was not implemented, vigilante groups did set up roadblocks in a haphazard way. Locals were warned to *not* dress up as gangsters for Halloween.

Still, as deadly as his spree became (some believe as many as 16 died by his hand alone), Dillinger won the hearts of many citizens. At the height of the Depression, he took on the persona of Robin Hood, sticking it to the fat cat bankers while acting with courtesy toward bystanders . . . as long as they behaved.

His brief, violent life still fascinates the public almost 70 years after his death at age 31 outside Chicago's Biograph Theater. So come along on a tour of Dillinger sites in the state he called home. But take the back roads and watch out for the coppers—they're everywhere, I tell ya—everywhere!

Indianapolis
John Dillinger's Birthplace

John Dillinger was born on June 22, 1903, in the Oak Hill neighborhood of Indianapolis. He was a normal baby, and did not emerge from the womb with guns a-blazing. At the time, Dillinger's father ran a grocery store (2210 Bloyd Ave., torn down) and was a deacon at Hillside Christian Church (1737 Ingram St.). John's mother, Mollie, died when he was only three years old. His father remarried, to a woman named Elizabeth Fields. John would always think of his stepmother as his mom.

There is little left of the Dillinger birthplace. A new home sits on the lot, but the curbside retaining wall is original. It's not hard to imagine little Johnnie playing marbles on the sidewalk along this wall.

Dillinger attended Public School No. 38 (Winter & Bloyd Aves.) just a block away, and later Public School No. 55 (17th & Sheldon Sts.). Both of these buildings are still standing.

Dillinger Birthplace, 2053 Caroline Ave. (formerly Cooper St.), Indianapolis, IN 46218

No phone

Hours: Torn down; a new home stands on the site

Cost: Free

Directions: Five blocks west of Keystone Way, just north of I-70.

Mooresville
John Dillinger's First Crime

The Dillinger family moved to Mooresville in March 1920, shortly before John turned 17. He joined the Navy in 1923, but turned back up in Mooresville five months later, AWOL from the USS *Utah*, docked in Boston.

Still "absent without leave" in 1924, Dillinger married a 16-year-old local woman, Beryl Hovious. He didn't seem interested in spending as much time with her as he did in a Mooresville poolroom with the guys. There he met up with Edgar Singleton, the resident hoodlum. Singleton enlisted Dillinger to help him mug a local grocer, Frank Morgan, on the night of September 6, 1924. The pair waited and drank in a niche near the side entrance to the Mooresville Christian Church. When Morgan passed by, walking home after closing, Singleton hit him over the head with a large bolt wrapped in a handkerchief. After being struck twice, the grocer got back up and smacked a gun out of Dillinger's hand, causing it to discharge. The pair got $150, but not for long.

Morgan gave the Masonic distress signal, which (along with the gunshot) woke the neighbors. The culprits ran off but were soon apprehended. Morgan could not positively identify Dillinger, though the cops tricked John into confessing with an empty promise of leniency. The judge sentencing Dillinger reneged on the offer and packed him off to jail for 10–20 years. Singleton pled "not guilty," his case went to trial, and he drew only 2–14 years.

Heritage Christian Church (former Mooresville Christian Church), 61 W. Harrison St.,
  Mooresville, IN 46158
Private phone
Hours: Always visible
Cost: Free
Directions: On the southeast corner of S. Jefferson and W. Harrison Sts.

The start of something big.

Michigan City
John Dillinger Learns the Trade

Dillinger's first prison home was the Indiana State Reformatory at Pendleton (4490 W. Reformatory Rd.), northeast of Indianapolis. Shortly after arriving, the new con tried to escape by hiding in a pile of excelsior, but was flushed out after the quick-thinking guards set fire to it.

Beryl divorced Dillinger while he was in prison. Not long after that, on July 25, 1929, he asked to be transferred to Indiana State Prison in Michigan City. Some say it was a move to mend his broken heart, but more likely it was because Michigan City had a better baseball team.

As Inmate #13225, he started hanging with a much rougher crowd. During his nine years of incarceration he joined in a plot for a massive prison break. According to the plan, the first conspirator released would launch weapons over the wall into the prison yard, to be retrieved by gang members still locked up. Those on the inside would then shoot their way out, if necessary.

Meanwhile, back in Mooresville, folks were trying to get Dillinger's harsh sentence reduced. Johnnie was eventually released on May 22, 1933, on an order signed by the governor. The governor had been persuaded by a petition signed by victim Frank Morgan (among others), and compassion for the imminent death of Dillinger's stepmother. As bad luck would have it, the ex-con arrived home only hours after she had died of a stroke.

Though there is no conclusive proof, many believe Dillinger tossed the weapons into the Michigan City prison that were eventually used by 10 inmates to escape on September 26, 1933. Their actions immediately following the break make that theory all the more convincing: they headed to Lima, Ohio, to spring Dillinger where *he* was then being held.

And how did he end up behind bars in Lima? That's the next part of the tour.

Indiana State Prison, 1 Park Row, Michigan City, IN 46360

(219) 874-7256

Hours: Always visible, view from street

Cost: Free

Directions: Where Chicago St. meets Hitchcock St.

Dillinger's First Crime Spree

When he wasn't working to spring his Big House buddies, Dillinger was robbing spots all over the Hoosier state. The first hit was less than a month after his release from Michigan City, and in less than four months he would be back behind bars.

Reader note: The events listed below reflect only *Indiana* crimes. Dillinger and his cohorts robbed many establishments around the Midwest. Additionally, there are more crimes attributed to Dillinger that he likely committed. Some could argue for additions or deletions to this list, but for the most part, these are definite Dillinger hits.

- **July 17, 1933:** Commercial Bank of Daleville (7850 Walnut St. **Daleville**; currently the Country Treasures furniture store). Assisted by Harry Copeland and Hilton Crouch, the trio was able to walk away with $3,500 from the Commercial Bank of Daleville. The former bank has a carved, split log over the old vault proclaiming "Dillinger Was Here."

- **August 4, 1933:** First National Bank of Montpelier (110 S. Main St., **Montpelier**; currently Pacesetter Financial Services). Copeland and Crouch were again involved in a Dillinger job that netted $10,110 and a .45 caliber gun. The gang headed to Bluffton, Ohio, for another bank heist before returning to the Hoosier state for a third hit.

- **September 6, 1933:** Massachusetts Avenue State Bank (Massachusetts Ave., **Indianapolis**). Dillinger, Copeland, and Crouch robbed the Indianapolis institution of $24,000. The bank was located near the then-headquarters of the Indiana State Police, and because of this false sense of security by proximity, security was lax. Some believe the gang buried the loot in Oak Hills, just west of town, and that it is still there for the finding.

Dillinger's Second Crime Spree

Dillinger was captured in Dayton, Ohio, on September 25, 1933, at the home of Mary Jenkins Longnacre, sister of jailhouse buddy Joseph Jenkins. At the time, he was carrying a map of the Michigan City Prison. The significance of the map became more apparent five days later when 10 armed inmates broke out of the facility. Officials didn't realize it at the time, but the gang was headed for the Allen County Jail in Lima, Ohio, to spring their helpful pal.

Meanwhile, Dillinger had confessed to robbing the Bluffton bank on August 14. His statement was never used in court since he was liberated by the outlaws on October 12. In the jailhouse shootout, Sheriff Jesse Sarber was killed.

Back in business, the Terror Gang's crime spree resumed operations two days later.

• **October 14, 1933:** Auburn Police Station Arsenal (9th & Cedar Sts., **Auburn**). Fresh out of prison and needing arms and ammunition, Harry Pierpoint, Walter Dietrich, and Dillinger marched into the Auburn police station arsenal (with guns drawn) and walked out with a Thompson submachine gun, eight other firearms, three bulletproof vests, and plenty of ammo.

• **October 21, 1933:** Peru Police Station Arsenal (3rd St. & Wabash, **Peru**). A week later, the same trio walked away with two Thompsons, eight other guns, a tear gas launcher, and six bulletproof vests from a police arsenal in Peru. The new police headquarters (35 S. Broadway) has one of the recovered machine guns on display in its lobby.

• **October 23, 1933:** Greencastle Central National Bank and Trust (20–24 W. Washington St., **Greencastle**). Unable to eat bullets, the Terror Gang planned an unauthorized cash withdrawal from a bank located on the southeast corner of Washington and Jackson Streets in Greencastle. Dillinger and seven others got $75,346, enough to keep them fed for a while. The gang headed for Daytona Beach and spent the New Year's holiday in the Florida sun.

• **January 15, 1934:** First National Bank (Indianapolis Blvd. & W. Chicago Ave., **East Chicago**). The first Hoosier holdup of 1934 took place at the First National Bank of East Chicago, netting $20,376. During their getaway, Dillinger shot and killed patrolman William

Patrick O'Malley with a machine gun. The gangster was also hit by gunfire, but he was wearing a bulletproof vest. John Hamilton and Harry Pierpont assisted Dillinger on the job.

Heeeeeere isn't Johnnie!

Crown Point
John Dillinger and the Wooden Gun
John Dillinger's bold exit from the Crown Point jail on March 3, 1934, established his persona as a coolheaded, confident hoodlum. However,

the tales surrounding the event are often fuzzy and inaccurate, from how he got there to how he escaped.

Here's what happened. Following the East Chicago job, Dillinger and company headed to the Southwest, ending up in Tucson, Arizona. The gang had just checked into the Congress Hotel on January 22, 1934, when the building caught fire. Flush with cash, they tipped the firemen who rescued their luggage a little too generously, raising suspicions. They were captured three days later. Though many states wanted him, Dillinger was extradited to Indiana on January 30 to face murder charges on the killing in East Chicago.

Dillinger was housed in the Crown Point Jail where he entertained a parade of private investigators, shifty lawyers, and fawning press. According to legend, he used his spare time to carve a wooden gun out of an old washboard, then coated it with shoe polish to make it look like a real pistol. Not true. More likely, the weapon was carved in Chicago and slipped to him by either a guard or private investigator Arthur O'Leary. Dillinger then dumped wood shavings in his cell to enhance his public image as a crafty fellow.

On March 3, Dillinger pulled the fake firearm on a guard in the second-floor exercise bullpen and, one by one, captured and incapacitated the jail's remaining officers and a civilian visitor, fingerprint expert Ernest Blunk. Assisted by murder suspect Herbert Youngblood, Dillinger stole two machine guns and a .45 not made of wood, and ducked out the rear kitchen entrance with "hostage" Blunk. He found Sheriff Lillian Holley's car in the Main Street Garage, two buildings north up East Street, and ordered the all-too-willing Blunk to act as getaway driver. The pair also took a mechanic from the garage, Edwin Saager.

The four headed west, but ran off the road at Lilley Corners, just east of Peotone, Illinois. It took half an hour to put chains on the tires and get the vehicle out of the ditch, yet Dillinger reportedly was calm through it all. He dumped Blunk and Saager near Peotone and gave them $4 for carfare back to Indiana. (Blunk would regret ever returning; he was eventually thrown in prison for being too helpful to the bank robber.) Youngblood and Dillinger then parted ways; Youngblood parted with the living two weeks later in a shootout in Port Huron, Michigan.

By crossing state lines to avoid capture, Dillinger committed a federal offense. The FBI became involved, and within months he earned the moniker of Public Enemy Number One. While Dillinger's reputation grew, Crown Point's image fell. The press dubbed the town Clown Point, and Republican politicos gleefully passed out souvenir wooden guns to mock Sheriff Holley, a Democratic elected official.

Today, the jail from which Dillinger escaped is a partially restored landmark open for occasional guided tours. The cells are still intact, but in miserable shape. While in Crown Point, be sure to visit the nearby Lake County Courthouse, where Ronald Reagan married Jane Wyman in 1923. This "Grand Old Lady of Lake County" was long used as a place to get a quick hitch, since they didn't require blood tests or have a waiting period. Rudolph Valentino, Joe DiMaggio, Red Grange, Tom Mix, and Muhammed Ali were also married here . . . though not to each other.

Old Sheriff's House, 228 S. Main St., PO Box 364, Crown Point, IN 46307

(219) 663-1800

Hours: Building always visible; call ahead for a tour

Cost: Adults $1, Kids 50¢

Directions: Two blocks south of the courthouse on the east side of Main St.

Lake County Courthouse Museum, 212 S. Main St., Crown Point, IN 46307

(219) 662-3975

Hours: May–October, Thursday–Saturday 1–4 P.M.

Cost: Adults $1, Kids 50¢

www.crownpoint.net

Directions: At Main and Joliet Sts.

Dillinger's Final Crime Spree

John Dillinger didn't spend too much time in his home state following his Crown Point escape, though he did return for two more heists . . . and a family reunion.

- **April 13, 1934:** Warsaw Police Station (121 N. Indiana St., **Warsaw**). Homer Van Meter helped Dillinger bump off his third Indiana police station. The pair got two handguns and three bulletproof vests. Today, the building houses the Kosciusko County Jail Museum (February–December, Thursday–Saturday 10 A.M.–4 P.M., Sunday 1–4 P.M., (574) 269-1078).

• June 30, 1934: Merchants National Bank, 229 N. Main St., **South Bend**).
In what would be his last Hoosier holdup, Dillinger, Van Meter, John
Paul Chase, and "Baby Face" Nelson hit the South Bend bank for over
$29,890. Van Meter killed policeman Howard Wagner in the process.

Mooresville
Dillinger Family Reunion

Amazing as it sounds, John Dillinger returned to Mooresville for a family
reunion on May 22, 1934, hiding out for a couple days in plain sight of
authorities. The whole clan got together for a two-day bash, and the
prodigal son was spotted walking around town. Dillinger posed with his
infamous wooden gun by the side of the house, then left the fake weapon
with his father.

Johnnie must have done some lobbying around town, because
residents soon began circulating a petition for the governor to pardon
Dillinger if the criminal promised to walk the straight and narrow.
The once-bitten governor didn't bite a second time, and the locals were
widely criticized for even *suggesting* such a plea bargain.

The FBI believes their Public Enemy Number One buried $600,000 in
stolen cash on his father's farm during the visit, but others put the loot's
sum closer to $1 million. It would be rather difficult to locate the cache
today, since the farmhouse was eventually torn down and the land turned
into a housing development.

Some people claim the ghosts of those who attended the picnic can
still be heard laughing on the get-together's May 22 anniversary date.
Others have smelled the odor of fried chicken.

Dillinger Farm, 535 Rte. 267, Mooresville, IN 46158

No phone

Hours: No longer there

Cost: Free

Directions: Where the housing development now stands, across from the EZ Way Rental
on the northwest end of town.

Indianapolis
John Dillinger's Grave

Two days after John Dillinger was gunned down outside Chicago's

Biograph Theater on July 22, 1934, his body was returned (minus its brain, which was removed for study) to his Indiana family. It first rested at the E. F. Harvey Funeral Home in Mooresville (now a frozen yogurt hut, Harrison & Indiana Sts.), then taken to the home of his sister, Audrey Hancock, in Maywood, just outside Indianapolis. The public viewing of its number one enemy halted after an hour, when a drunken admirer tried to give Johnnie a swig from his flask.

Dillinger's father was offered $10,000 by a traveling sideshow for his son's body, but didn't accept the offer. The hucksters insisted the fee was just to *rent* the corpse, and that the Dillingers would eventually get it back. Yeah, that's what the FBI said about his brain. . . .

The gangster's grave was lined with a three-foot thick concrete vault to discourage grave robbers. Headstone robbers would find things a little easier; his gravestone has been stolen four times (to date) and its popularity shows no sign of waning.

Crown Hill Cemetery, 700 W. 38th St., Indianapolis, IN 46208

(317) 925-8231 or (317) 920-2644 (Tours)

Hours: April–September, daily 8 A.M.–6 P.M.; October–March, daily 8 A.M.–5 P.M.

Cost: Free; Heritage Tours, Adults $5, Seniors $4, Kids $3

www.crownhill.org

Directions: Bound by 32nd St., Boulevard Pl., 38th St., and Northwestern Ave. Enter from 3402 Boulevard Place.

PARTNERS IN CRIME

What happened to the other members of the Terror Gang? Most ended up like Dillinger: dead. **Harry Pierpont** was executed in the Ohio electric chair on October 17, 1934, and buried in Indianapolis's Holy Cross Cemetery (435 W. Troy Ave.). **Homer Van Meter** was gunned down by police officers in St. Paul, Minnesota, on August 23, 1934. He is planted in Fort Wayne's Lindenwood Cemetery (2324 W. Main St.). **Charles Mackley** died in a botched prison escape on March 27, 1934, while awaiting execution in Ohio. He was reported to have once claimed, "I'd rather take the hot squat than see Johnnie caught." He never had to make the choice.

Dillinger's Guns

Many of the guns Dillinger used in his crime sprees were taken from Hoosier law enforcement officials. It seems only appropriate that the main police museum in the state might get some of them back, but the Indiana State Police Historical Museum's collection spends less time on their greatest foe than you might think—perhaps there's still a little bad blood. They do have one corner with a few firearms, a bulletproof vest, a replica of the wooden pistol, Johnnie's death mask, a mannequin handing over some ill-gotten money, one of the gangster's many stolen headstones, and other Dillinger-abilia.

This museum also has a large stash of bongs and crack pipes, uniforms and squad cars, confiscated jailhouse weaponry, radar guns, smashed slot machines and stills, and Drunkometers. Be sure to bring a camera to get a gag "head-cutout" photo of yourself as a jewel thief, nabbed by the ever vigilant Indiana State Police. Crime does not pay! At least not forever . . .

Indiana State Police Historical Museum, 8500 E. 21st St., Indianapolis, IN 46219

(317) 899-8293

Hours: Monday–Friday 8–11 A.M., 1–4 P.M.

Cost: Free

www.in.gov/isp

Directions: Two blocks east of Post Rd., just south of I-70.

Hammond
Dillinger Museum

So you say you don't have the time to run around the state looking at crumbling banks, jails, and police stations. That's where the John Dillinger Museum comes in handy—one-stop shopping for the crimeophile. Sponsored by the Lake County Convention and Visitors Bureau, this fascinating hands-on collection is probably the most entertaining museum in the state. Surprisingly, the curators are not shy about their county's association with the most embarrassing tale in the Dillinger saga, the Crown Point jailbreak, but give accurate and complete information, even if it hurts.

The museum is arranged chronologically, according to Dillinger's life. You start by visiting John's early years on the farm, then BAM! you're in prison. The small cell and looped recording of an angry guard have a distinctly *Oz*-like feel. Judge for yourself whether Dillinger's sentence fit the Mooresville crime with an interactive game. Once in prison, see the faces of the Terror Gang formed in Michigan City.

Next, follow the gang's crime spree as a witness to the East Chicago holdup—see how many details you can remember after staring down the barrel of a gun. Check out the 1933 Essex Terraplane, Dillinger's getaway car of choice. See a replica of the wooden gun that fooled Crown Point officials. (The original gun is part of the museum's collection, but is too valuable to put on display.)

Do you think a life of crime might be a glamorous career option? Think again—the next exhibit is an FBI lab, where you are fingerprinted and booked. View the aftermath of the Little Bohemia shootout, and the bloody end for Dillinger and the gang. The final, shocking displays include Johnnie's "pants of death," a bleeding wax dummy of Johnnie on the Cook County morgue's autopsy slab, and the undertaker's basket used to transport his body.

Scattered throughout the museum are dummies of other Depression-era hoodlums, like Pretty Boy Floyd, Baby Face Nelson, Ma Barker, and Bonnie and Clyde, all of whom died of acute lead poisoning.

7770 Corinne Dr., Hammond, IN 46323

(800) ALL-LAKE (255-5253) or (219) 989-7770

Hours: Daily 9 A.M.–6 P.M.

Cost: Adults $4, Seniors (55+) $3, Kids (under 12) $3

www.dillingermuseum.homestead.com

Directions: Take the Kennedy Ave. Exit south from I-80/94, turn west at the first light.

Goshen
Bank Robbers Beware!

In a move akin to shutting the barn door after the cows got out, the city of Goshen erected a bulletproof police booth along the transcontinental Lincoln Highway . . . five years after Dillinger was laid to rest in an Indianapolis cemetery. The octagonal limestone watchpost was built by the WPA at a busy intersection in sight of several banks, and it had gun portholes and impenetrable glass.

The booth was in 24-hour use until 1969; and though some laughed at their over-the-top effort, while it was in operation no bank robberies occurred at any nearby Goshen institutions.

Main St. & Lincoln Ave., Goshen, IN 46528

No phone

Hours: Always visible

Cost: Free

Directions: On the southeast corner of the courthouse square, on Rte. 33.

Ready for anything.

EPiLOGUe

OK, thank God for small favors, but what else have you missed out on? Indianapolis was once home to some interesting architecture, like the ship-shaped Barge Fish 'N' Chips that stood at Washington & Denny Streets, the Polk Sanitary Milk Building with its two white bottle towers on 15th Street, and the TeePee Restaurant on Fall Creek Boulevard. All are gone. Austin's two-story Coffee Pot Restaurant and Filling Station percolated its last cup in 1960, much as the Frozen Custard Igloo in Lafayette had a dozen years earlier, and The Barrel in South Bend.

Attractions associated with Hoosier factories have not fared well, closing when the industries moved elsewhere. Noble County once manufactured more than half of the world's marshmallows, but the tours stopped when the last of the plants moved to Ohio. Ligonier's annual Marshmallow Festival is now on squishy ground. Seyfert Foods of Fort Wayne had Myrtle Young's collection of 400 famous potato chips. Working as a picker on the chip line, Young discovered likenesses of Tweetie Bird, Mr. Magoo, Bob Hope, Rodney Dangerfield, Yogi Bear, and Ronald Reagan and had exhibited them on the *Tonight Show*. But when the plant moved to Missouri, so did her unique collection. And Jeffersonville was long home to baseball's Slugger Park, located adjacent to the milling operations for the Louisville Slugger, but the park disappeared when the outfit moved across the river to, of all places, Louisville.

Some oddball sites have fallen victim to bad PR. The American Atheist Museum in Petersburg, which sponsored Dial-an-Atheist and billed itself as "(t)he most ungodly place north of the Mason-Dixon line," was probably doomed from the start. The International Palace of Sports in North Webster crowned a King of Sports each year and reproduced the honored athlete in wax. As bad luck would have it, one of its first Kings was O. J. Simpson. The castle-shaped building is a discount shoe outlet today. And Hy Goldenberg's Outhouse Collection in Huntington didn't draw nearly as many visitors as the town's Dan Quayle Museum . . . if you can believe it.

Who knows what happened to some roadside oddities? Where did the Brazen Serpent of Bedford go? The 21-foot-long, 300-pound, hand-carved snake had 362 wooden ribs and 4,000 metal scales and would hiss at visitors, powered from within by a small motor. Only one building from Chesterton's 125-piece Littleville survives (in the backyard of a local resident), but the other 124 have to be *somewhere*, don't they? And the Martinsville structure that once housed Drake's Midwest Phonograph Museum of more than 600 recording devices is now a church. There are already plenty of those around, but where can you find a machine that records sound on chocolate? Not Martinsville.

Heed my warning, fellow travelers! The evil forces of good taste are wiping out unique and bizarre attractions wherever they find them. Indiana is no exception. There was a time, not so long ago, that the present oh-so-precious town of Nashville had both a Dillinger Museum and a Serpentarium crammed with venomous snakes and photos of humans who'd been bitten. Just try and find something, *anything*, that wonderful in Nashville today.

So go. GO! The oddballs are out there—but they won't be forever. In a world of round donuts, can you live with the knowledge that you passed up an opportunity to eat a square one? I can't.

ACKNOWLEDGMENTS

*I*ndiana is a wonderful state. I know because I spent four years of my life in South Bend. Some of the nicest folks I've ever known lived there, and still do. But I also had the misfortune of being in South Bend on January 20, 1985, when the wind chill dropped to minus 80 degrees—a new state record—and I swore to myself that when I left that town I would never return. Ever.

Well, it's difficult to hold a Canadian cold front against an entire state, and when the snow melted that spring, so did my resolve. I did leave, yet the first three-day road trip I ever took in search of oddball sites was back through Hoosierland; and I've returned dozens of times over the years for day trips and extended vacations. The end result is this travel guide.

This book would not have been possible without the assistance, patience, and good humor of many individuals. My thanks go out to the following people for allowing me to interview them about their roadside attractions: Bill Arnold (Wire America), Linda Black (Jim Jones's Early Life), "Blondie" (Murat Temple), Hazel Carter (Quilters Hall of Fame), Mabel Gray (Museum of All Sorts of Stuff), Hartley Funeral Home in Arcadia (Ryan White's Grave), Al Hesselbart (RV/MH Heritage Foundation), Andrea Hill (West Baden Springs Hotel), Keith Kaiser (Dan Quayle Childhood Home), Rick Kiefer (National New York Central Railroad Museum), Yvonne Knight (Howard Steamboat Museum), Becky Lindquist (RV/MH Heritage Foundation), Roselyn McKittrick (*Hoosiers/* Milan Station Antiques & Collectibles), Jean Nelson (Oz Museum), Sally Newkirk (Yenawine Exhibit), Betty Palmer (Willard Library), Maria Peacock (Bendix Woods), Susan Richter (Belle Gunness/La Porte County Historical Society Museum), DeVon Rose (Bird's-Eye View Museum), C. R. Schiefer (Touchables Sculpture Garden), Julia Stolle (Museum of Miniature Houses), Katie Stone (Howard Steamboat Museum), Virginia

Terpening (Indiana Medical History Museum), Ted Waflart (Dr. Ted's Musical Marvels), Peter Youngman (Diana of the Dunes/Ogden Dunes Historical Society), and Gaby Zimmerman (Bill Monroe's Memorial Music Park & Campground).

For research assistance, I am indebted to the librarians in the Indiana communities of Carmel, Chesterton, Crawfordsville, Daleville, Evansville, Freetown, Gosport, Greensburg, Jasper, Martinsville, Monticello, Montpelier, Mooresville, New Carlisle, Odon, Peru, Seymour, Shoals, South Bend, Tell City, Terre Haute, and Winamac. Thanks also to the Visitors Bureaus and/or Chambers of Commerce in Bedford, Bloomington, Columbus, Fort Wayne, Huntington, Indianapolis, Madison, Muncie, Nashville, New Albany, New Harmony, Porter, Richmond, Seymour, Vevay, and Warsaw. I was also assisted by the Santa Claus post office and the *Curubusco News*.

Friends and family members willingly volunteered (sometimes after excessive badgering on my part) to act as models for the photographs in this book: Jim Frost, Gianofer Fields, Patrick Hughes, Eugene Marceron, James & Naomi Lane, Yoshio & Yukiko Sakamoto, Eriko Sakamoto, and Richard Lane. You were all great sports.

My deep gratitude to everyone at Chicago Review Press (many of whom are Hoosiers!) for supporting the Oddball travel series. To the folks at WBEZ, Chicago Public Radio, particularly Gianofer Fields and Cate Cahan, thank you for the opportunity to bring these stories to your listeners.

To the Hoosiers (native, adopted, or temporary) in my life, Olga, Tom, Kyle, and Taylor Granat, James & Naomi Lane, Elizabeth Wangler, and Maggie Gomer, I hope I did your state justice. To my Notre Dame friends through the Center for Social Concerns, especially Kathy Royer, Mary Ann Roemer, Dee Schlotfeldt, Don McNeill, and Eugene McClory, when I think of Indiana, I think of you, and I forget all about 80 below.

Finally, to Jim Frost, who has driven with me to the moon and back in my Saturn, my deepest gratitude.

RECOMMENDED SOURCES

If you'd like to learn more about the places and individuals in this book, the following are excellent sources.

Introduction
General Indiana Guides
Indiana: A New Historical Guide by Robert Taylor, Errol Wayne Stevens, Mary Ann Ponder, and Paul Brockman (Indianapolis: Indiana Historical Society, 1989)

Indiana Historical Tour Guide by D. Ray Wilson (Carpentersville, IL: Crossroads Communications, 1994)

Indiana Off the Beaten Path by Phyllis Thomas (Old Saybrook, CT: Globe Pequot Press, 1998)

Indiana Legends by Nelson Price (Carmel, IN: Guild Press of Indiana, 1997)

Amazing Tales from Indiana by Fred Cavinder (Bloomington, IN: Indiana University Press, 1990)

Borderline Indiana by Wendell Trogdon (Mooresville, IN: Backroads Press, 1996)
Indiana Trivia
Awesome Almanac: Indiana by Jean Blasfield (Fontana, WI: B & B Publishing, Inc., 1993)

The Indiana Book of Records, Firsts, and Fascinating Facts by Fred Cavinder (Bloomington, IN: Indiana University Press, 1985)

Indiana Trivia by Ernie and Jill Crouch (Nashville, TN: Rutledge Hill Press, 1997)

Legends and Losers by Andy Jones (South Bend, IN: and books, 1999)

From Needmore to Prosperity: Hoosier Place Names in Folklore and History by Ronald Baker (Bloomington, IN: Indiana University Press, 1995)
Indiana Ghosts
Hoosier Hauntings by K. T. MacRorie (Grand Rapids, MI: Thunder Bay Press, 1997)

Haunted Indiana by Mark Marimen (Grand Rapids, MI: Thunder Bay Press, 1997)

1. Northern Indiana

Auburn Cord Duesenberg Museum

It's a Duesy! by Lee P. Sauer (Auburn, IN: Auburn Cord Duesenberg Museum, 1999)

Oz Museum

The Munchkins of Oz by Stephen Cox (Nashville, TN: Cumberland House, 1996)

The Lincoln Highway's "Ideal Section"

The Lincoln Highway Forum (Tucson, AZ: Lincoln Highway Association)

RVs and Motor Homes

Home on the Road: The Motor Home in America by Roger B. White (Washington, DC: Smithsonian Institution Press, 2000)

Johnny Appleseed

Johnny Appleseed: Man and Myth by Robert Price (Bloomington, IN: Indiana University Press, 1954)

Octave Chanute

Progress in Flying Machines by Octave Chanute and Adam Frost (New York: Dover Publications, 1998)

The Jackson 5

Michael Jackson: The Magic and the Madness by J. Randy Taraborrelli (New York: Birch Lane Press, 1991)

Michael Unauthorized by Christopher Andersen (New York: Simon & Schuster, 1994)

Dan Quayle

The Man Who Would Be President by Bob Woodward and David S. Broder (New York: Simon & Schuster, 1992)

Standing Firm by Dan Quayle (New York: HarperCollins, 1994)

What a Waste It Is to Lose One's Mind from *The Quayle Quarterly* (Bridgeport, CT: *The Quayle Quarterly*, 1992)

The Dan Quayle Quiz Book by Jeremy Solomon and Ken Brady (Boston: Little, Brown & Company, 1989)

Belle Gunness

The Gunness Story by Madeline G. Kinney and Gretchen Tyler (La Porte, IN: La Porte County Historical Society, 1984)

Lodner Phillips and His Submarines

Great Lakes' First Submarine by Patricia A. Gruse Harris (Michigan City, IN: Michigan City Historical Society, 1982)

Indiana Circuses

Life in a Three-Ring Circus by Sharon Smith and Stephen J. Fletcher (Indianapolis, IN: Indiana University Press, 2001)

Indiana's Big Top by Don L. Chaffee (Grand Rapids, MI: Foremost Press, 1969)

The First 25 Years by DeLoris Welden (Peru, IN: Circus City Festival, Inc., 1985)

Cole Porter

Cole Porter: A Biography by William McBrien (New York: Alfred A. Knopf, 1998)

Elmo Lincoln, the First Tarzan

My Father, Elmo Lincoln, The Original Tarzan by Marci'a Lincoln Rudolph (Rochester, IN: self-published, date unknown)

Studebaker

More than They Promised: The Studebaker Story by Thomas E. Bonsall (Palo Alto, CA: Stanford University Press, 2000)

Studebaker: The Life and Death of an American Corporation by Donald Critchclow (Bloomington, IN: Indiana University Press, 1997)

George Gipp

One for the Gipper by Patrick Chellan (New York: Arrowhead Classics, 1996)

2. Central Indiana

The Battle of Tippecanoe

Sorrow in Our Heart: The Life of Tecumseh by Allan W. Eckert (New York: Bantam Books, 1996)

Old Tippecanoe: William Henry Harrison and His Time by Freeman Cleeves (American Political Biography Press, 1990)

Jim Jones and the People's Temple

White Night by John Peer Nugent (New York: Rawson, Wade Publishers, Inc., 1979)

Our Father Who Art in Hell by James Reston, Jr. (New York: *Times* Books, 1981)

James Dean

James Dean: The Mutant King by David Dalton (Chicago: A Cappella, 2001)

Boulevard of Broken Dreams by Paul Alexander (New York: Viking, 1994)

The James Dean Story by Ronald Martinetti (New York: Birch Lane Press, 1995)

Levi Coffin and the Underground Railroad

Levi Coffin: Quaker Breaking the Bonds of Slavery in Ohio and Indiana by Mary Ann Yannessa (Richmond, IN: Friends United Press, 2001)

Reminiscences of Levi Coffin: The Reputed President of the Underground Railroad by Levi Coffin and Ben Richmond (Richmond, IN: Friends United Press, 2001)

Ryan White
My Own Story by Ryan White and Ann Marie Cunningham (New York: Dial
   Books, 1991)
The Real Hoosiers
The Greatest Basketball Story Ever Told by Greg Guffy (Bloomington, IN: Indiana
   University Press, 1993)

3. Southern Indiana
Bill Monroe
Can't You Hear Me Callin': The Life of Bill Monroe, the Father of Bluegrass by
   Richard D. Smith (Boston: Little, Brown & Company, 2000)
Bobby Knight
A Season on the Brink: A Year with Bob Knight and the Indiana Hoosiers by John
   Feinstein (New York: MacMillan, 1996)
Knight Fall by Phil Berger (New York: Pinnacle Books, 2000)
Kinsey Institute
Sex the Measure of All Things: A Life of Alfred C. Kinsey by Jonathan Gathorne-
   Hardy (Bloomington, IN: Indiana University Press, 2000)
Peek: Photographs from the Kinsey Insitute by Carol Squiers (Santa Fe, NM: Arena
   Editions, 2000)
Lincoln in Indiana
Lincoln's Youth by Louis Warren (Indianapolis: Indiana Historical Society, 1991)
New Harmony
Walker's Guide to New Harmony's History by Janet R. Walker (New Harmony, IN:
   Historic New Harmony, 1996)
New West Baden Springs Hotel
History of the New West Baden Springs Hotel by Gregory S. Gatsos (West Baden
   Springs, IN: self-published, 2001)
West Baden Springs: Legacy of Dreams by Chris Bundy (West Baden Springs, IN:
   self-published, 2001)

4. Indianapolis Area
David Letterman
The Letterman Wit by Bill Adler (New York: Carroll & Graff Publishers, Inc., 1994)
David Letterman by Frances Lefkowitz (New York: Chelsea House, 1997)
Dave's World by Michael Cader (New York: Warner Books, 1995)

Mike Tyson

Heavy Justice: The Trial of Mike Tyson by Randy Roberts and J. Gregory Garrison
(New York: Addison Wesley, 1994)

USS Indianapolis

Abandon Ship! by Richard F. Newcomb (New York: HarperCollins, 2001)

In Harm's Way: The Sinking of the USS Indianapolis *and the Extraordinary Story of Its Survivors* by Doug Stanton (New York: Henry Holt & Company, 2001)

Indy 500

Indianapolis 500 Chronicle by Rick Popely (Lincolnwood, IL: Publications International, 1998)

5. Dillinger Diapers-to-Death Tour

Dillinger: A Short and Violent Life by Rober Cromie and Joseph Pinkston
(Evanston, IL: Chicago Historical Bookworks, 1990)

Dillinger: The Untold Story by G. Russell Girardin and William J. Hemmler
(Bloomington, IN: Indiana University Press, 1994)

The Dillinger Days by John Tollard (Cambridge, MA: Da Capo Press, 1995)

Dillinger Strikes in East Chicago by Richard Smyers (self-published: East Chicago Public Library, date unknown)

INDEX BY CITY NAME

Alamo
America's Least-Dead Revolutionary Soldier, 58

Amity
Nancy Barnett Isn't Moving!, 59

Angola
Lottery Bowl, 2

Auburn
Auburn Cord Duesenberg Museum, 2

Avon
Dead Dad Jones, 184

Battle Ground
Tippecanoe Battlefield Monument, 60
Wolf Park, 61

Bean Blossom
Bill Monroe Country Star Museum & Campground, 112

Bedford
Bluespring Caverns, 132
Foote's Tomb and the Bedford Cemetery, 113

Beverly Shores
House of Tomorrow, The, 3

Bloomington
Bobby Knight Meets Zero Tolerance, 114
Breaking Away, 116
George Washington and the Prime Directive (Lilly Library of Rare Books and Manuscripts), 117
Kinsey Institute for Research in Sex, Gender, and Reproduction, 118
Midwestern Tibet, 120

Bremen
World's Fattest Man Death Site, 4

Bruceville
Giant Peach, 121

Bryant

Wrenching Barn, A, 62

Cairo

Eyes to the Skies!, 63

Cannelton

Finding Out the Hard Way (Electra Crash Memorial), 158

Carmel

Illusions, 186

Museum of Miniature Houses and Other Collections, 186

World's First Traffic Light (Carmel-Clay Historical Society), 187

Chesterfield

Spiritualist Camp (Camp Chesterfield), 64

Chesterton

Diana of the Dunes (Ogden Dunes), 5

Oz Museum, The (Yellow Brick Road Gift Shop), 7

Churubusco

Oscar, the Beast of 'Busco, 8

Cicero

Ryan White's Real Hometown and Grave, 65

Clarksville

Mad, Mad Mary Kay Lady (Crouch's Body Shop & Frame Work), 122

World's Second Largest Clock, 124

Cloverdale

House of Bells, 66

Columbus

Birthplace of Corn Flakes, 124

Corydon

Squire Boone Caverns and Village, 132

Crawfordsville

Ben Hur Museum (Lew Wallace Study), 67

Old Jail Museum, 67

Crete

Jim Jones's Birthplace, 68

Crown Point

John Dillinger and the Wooden Gun (Old Sheriff's House), 197

Dale

Dr. Ted's Musical Marvels, 125

Dunns Bridge

Remains of the World's First Ferris Wheel, 9

Dyer

"Ideal Section" and the Ostermann Bench, The, 10

East Chicago

Park on the Sidewalk, Walk in the Street, 12

Elkhart

Birthplace of Alka-Seltzer, 13

Curly Top and the Toothpick Train (New York Central Museum), 14

RV/MH Heritage Foundation/Hall of Fame, 15

Evansville

Lady in Gray (Willard Library), The, 126

Fairmount

Fairmount High School, 71

Fairmount Historical Museum, 74

James Dean Memorial Gallery, 75

James Dean's Boyhood Home, 71

James Dean's Grave, 73

Fort Wayne

"Fish Eaters and Idol Worshippers" (Cathedral Museum), 16

Johnny Appleseed's Grave, 17

Lincoln Museum, 18

Philo T. Farnsworth TV Museum, 20

Fountain City

Grand Central Station on the Underground Railroad (Levi Coffin House), 76

Gary

Gary, First in Flight, 20

Jackson 5 Sites, 22

Geneva

Amishville, U.S.A., 25

Goshen

Bank Robbers Beware!, 203

Gosport

Chivalry Trough, The, 128

Greencastle
Buzz Bomb, 77
Dan Quayle's Frat House, 78
Greenfield
Old Crow, The, 79
Greensburg
Tree on the Courthouse, 80
Hammond
Dillinger Museum, 202
Highland
Devil, Be Gone! (Hegewisch Baptist Church), 27
Hindustan
Don't Sit in the Witch's Chair! (Stepp Cemetery), 130
Huntington
Dan Quayle Center and Museum, 28
Real Quayle Trail, The, 28
Indianapolis
Birthplace of Wonder Bread, 170
Daniel Boone, Tree Vandal (Eagle Creek Park), 171
David Letterman, Bag Boy (Atlas Supermarket), 172
Dillinger's Guns (Indiana State Police Museum), 202
Elvis's Last Concert (Market Square Arena), 173
Hannah House, 174
Indiana Medical History Museum, 174
Indiana Walk of Legends (Indiana State Fairgrounds), 175
John Dillinger's Birthplace, 192
John Dillinger's Grave (Crown Hill Cemetery), 200
King Tut and the Scots (Murat Temple and the Ancient Order of the Scottish Rite), 176
Mega-Popcorn Blast (Pepsi Coliseum), 177
Mike Tyson Gets into Trouble (Canterbury Hotel), 178
Original People's Temple, The, 179
Sleep in a Train (Crowne Plaza Union Station), 181
USS *Indianapolis* Memorial, 182
World's Largest Trowel, 183
Jasper
Geode Garden, 131

Jeffersonville
Bridge That Goes Nowhere, The, 134
Howard Steamboat Museum, 135
Kendallville
Mid-America Windmill Museum, 33
Knightstown
William Arnold, Truck Stop Artist, 81
Kokomo
Ryan White's Former Home, 83
World's First Automobile (Elwood Haynes Museum), 84
World's Largest Steer and World's Largest Sycamore Stump, 86
Lafayette
Pizza King, 87
Rainforest Car Wash, 89
La Porte
Belle Was a Groundbreaker (La Porte County Historical Society Museum), 34
Leopold
Thou Shall Not Steal (Shrine of Our Lady of Consolation), 136
Ligonier
Indiana Historical Radio Museum, 36
Lincoln City
Don't Drink the Milk! (Lincoln Boyhood National Monument), 137
Logansport
Catch the Brass Ring (Cass County Carousel), 37
Lynn
Jim Jones's Childhood Home, 68
Marengo
Marengo Cave, 133
Martinsville
Clown Heaven, 138
Touchables Sculpture Garden, The, 139
Marion
James Dean's Birthplace, 91
Mentone
World's Largest Egg, 38

Michigan City
John Dillinger Learns the Trade (Michigan City Prison), 194
Submarine Superstar (Lighthouse Museum), 40
Milan
Real *Hoosiers*, The, 91
Milltown
Shoe Tree, 141
Mitchell
Virgil I. Grissom State Memorial (Spring Mill State Park), 142
Mooresville
Dillinger Family Reunion, 200
John Dillinger's First Crime, 192
Morgantown
Rock House Inn, 143
Muncie
Barfly Cortez and the Lumberjack, 93
David Letterman, C Student (Ball State), 94
Munster
Carmelite Shrines, 41
Nappanee
Amish Acres, 25
Needmore
Cursed Pyramid and Crumbling Wall of China, 144
New Albany
Yenawine Exhibit (Carnegie Center for Art and History), 145
New Carlisle
World's Largest Living Sign (Bendix Woods), 42
New Castle
Big Sneaker (Steve Alford All-American Inn), 95
New Harmony
Angel Gabriel's Footprints (Rapp-Maclure Home), The, 146
New Harmony Labyrinth, 147
Oolitic
Big Palooka, A, 148
Orangeville
Lost River and the Orangeville Rise, The, 149

Oxford
Dan Patch, Gone, 95
Peru
Circus Museum, 43
Cole Porter's Birthplace and Grave, 44
Freaks of Nature, and Cole Porter's Hand-Me-Downs (Miami County Museum), 45
Plainfield
Dump the President! (Van Buren Elm), 188
Pumpkin Center
Museum of All Sorts of Stuff, The, 150
Richmond
Keeping Up with the Joneses, 97
Rochester
Hoosier Tarzan (Fulton County Round Museum), 46
Roselawn
Hanging Out in Roselawn (Sun Aura & Ponderosa Sun Ranch), 47
Russiaville
Ryan White, Pariah (Western Middle School), 83
St. Leon
Hickory Pole, The, 79
Santa Claus
Holiday World, 152
Santa Claus Town, 153
Seymour
America's First Train Robbery, 155
Shipshewana
Menno-Hof Mennonite-Amish Visitors Center, 26
South Bend
Studebaker National Museum and Archives, 48
Where the Gipper Croaked (Notre Dame/Washington Hall), 49
Speedway
Speedway and the Hall of Fame Museum, The, 189
Spencer
Big Chicken (Owen County Fairgrounds), 157
Stone Head
Stone Head, 157

Tell City
Finding Out the Hard Way (Electra Victim Graves), 158
Terre Haute
Birthplace of the Curvaceous Coke Bottle (Vigo County Museum), 98
Chuck, Tim, and the Unabomber, 99
Square Donuts, 100
Stiffy Green, the Stiff Dog (Highland Cemetery, Vigo County Museum), 101
World's First Pay Toilets, 103
Thorntown
Crown of Thorntown (Garden of Memories), 103
Union City
Towns Torn in Half, 104
Valparaiso
New Way of Spelling, A, 50
Vandalia
Barn House, The, 159
Vevay
Mary Wright's Creepy Piano (Switzerland County Historical Museum), 160
Vincennes
Trigger-Happy Warship, 162
Wakarusa
Bird's-Eye View Museum, 50
Warsaw
Biblical Gardens, 52
Hallmark Ornament Museum, 52
West Baden Springs
New West Baden Springs Hotel, The, 163
West College Corner
Towns Torn in Half, 104
Windfall
Michael Craig Sculpture Garden, 105
Worthington
Remnants of the World's Largest Deciduous Tree, 165
Wyandotte
Wyandotte Cave, 134
Yorktown
Big Jack, 106

INDEX BY Site Name

America's First Train Robbery, 155

America's Least-Dead Revolutionary Soldier, 58

Amish Acres, 25

Amishville, U.S.A., 25

Angel Gabriel's Footprints, The (Rapp-Maclure Home), 146

Auburn Cord Duesenberg Museum, 2

Bank Robbers Beware!, 203

Barfly Cortez and the Lumberjack, 93

Barn House, The, 159

Bedford Cemetery, 113

Belle Was a Groundbreaker (La Porte County Historical Society Museum), 34

Ben Hur Museum (Lew Wallace Study), 67

Biblical Gardens, 52

Big Chicken (Owen County Fairgrounds), 157

Big Jack, 106

Big Palooka, A, 148

Big Sneaker (Steve Alford All-American Inn), 95

Bill Monroe Country Star Museum & Campground, 112

Bird's-Eye View Museum, 50

Birthplace of Alka-Seltzer, 13

Birthplace of Corn Flakes, 124

Birthplace of the Curvaceous Coke Bottle (Vigo County Museum), 98

Birthplace of Wonder Bread, 170

Bluespring Caverns, 132

Bobby Knight Meets Zero Tolerance, 114

Breaking Away, 116

Bridge That Goes Nowhere, The, 134

Buzz Bomb, 77

Carmelite Shrines, 41

Catch the Brass Ring (Cass County Carousel), 37

Chivalry Trough, The, 128

Chuck, Tim, and the Unabomber, 99

Circus Museum, 43

Clown Heaven, 138

Cole Porter's Birthplace and Grave, 44

Crown of Thorntown (Garden of Memories), 103

Curly Top and the Toothpick Train (New York Central Museum), 14

Cursed Pyramid and Crumbling Wall of China, 144

Dan Patch, Gone, 96

Dan Quayle Center and Museum, 28

Dan Quayle's Frat House, 78

Daniel Boone, Tree Vandal (Eagle Creek Park), 171

David Letterman, Bag Boy (Atlas Supermarket), 172

David Letterman, C Student (Ball State), 94

Dead Dad Jones, 184

Devil, Be Gone! (Hegewisch Baptist Church), 27

Diana of the Dunes (Ogden Dunes), 5

Dillinger Family Reunion, 200

Dillinger Museum, 202

Dillinger's Final Crime Spree, 199

Dillinger's First Crime Spree, 195

Dillinger's Second Crime Spree, 195

Dillinger's Guns (Indiana State Police Museum), 202

Dr. Ted's Musical Marvels, 125

Don't Drink the Milk! (Lincoln Boyhood National Monument), 137

Don't Sit in the Witch's Chair! (Stepp Cemetery), 130

Dump the President! (Van Buren Elm), 188

Elvis's Last Concert (Market Square Arena), 173

Eyes to the Skies!, 63

Fairmount High School, 71

Fairmount Historical Museum, 74

Finding Out the Hard Way (Electra Crash Memorial and Victim's Graves), 158

"Fish Eaters and Idol Worshippers" (Cathedral Museum), 16

Foote's Tomb, 113

Freaks of Nature & Cole Porter's Hand-Me-Downs (Miami County Museum), 45

Gary, First in Flight, 20

Geode Garden, 131

George Washington and the Prime Directive (Lilly Library of Rare Books and Manuscripts), 117

Giant Peach, 121

Grand Central Station on the Underground Railroad (Levi Coffin House), 76

Hallmark Ornament Museum, 52

Hanging Out in Roselawn (Sun Aura & Ponderosa Sun Ranch), 47

Hannah House, 174

Hickory Pole, The, 79

Holiday World, 152

Hoosier Tarzan (Fulton County Round Museum), 46

House of Bells, 66

House of Tomorrow, The, 3

Howard Steamboat Museum, 135

"Ideal Section" and the Ostermann Bench, The, 10

Illusions, 186

Indiana Historical Radio Museum, 36

Indiana Medical History Museum, 174

Indiana Walk of Legends (Indiana State Fairgrounds), 175

Jackson 5 Sites, 22

James Dean Memorial Gallery, 75

James Dean's Birthplace, 91

James Dean's Boyhood Home, 71

James Dean's Grave, 73

Jim Jones's Birthplace, 68

Jim Jones's Childhood Home, 68

John Dillinger and the Wooden Gun (Old Sheriff's House), 197

John Dillinger Learns the Trade (Michigan City Prison), 194

John Dillinger's Birthplace, 192

John Dillinger's First Crime, 192

John Dillinger's Grave (Crown Hill Cemetery), 200

Johnny Appleseed's Grave, 17

Keeping Up with the Joneses, 97

King Tut and the Scots (Murat Temple and the Ancient Order of the Scottish Rite), 176

Kinsey Institute for Research in Sex, Gender, and Reproduction, 118

Lady in Gray, The (Willard Library), 126

Lincoln Museum, 18

Lost River and the Orangeville Rise, The, 149

Lottery Bowl, 2

Mad, Mad Mary Kay Lady (Crouch's Body Shop & Frame Work), 122

Marengo Cave, 133

Mary Wright's Creepy Piano (Switzerland County Historical Museum), 160

Mega-Popcorn Blast (Pepsi Coliseum), 177

Menno-Hof Mennonite-Amish Visitors Center, 26

Michael Craig Sculpture Garden, 105

Mid-America Windmill Museum, 33

Midwestern Tibet, 120

Mike Tyson Gets into Trouble (Canterbury Hotel), 178

Museum of All Sorts of Stuff, The, 150

Museum of Miniature Houses and Other Collections, 186

Nancy Barnett Isn't Moving!, 59

New Harmony Labyrinth, 147

New Way of Spelling, A, 50

New West Baden Springs Hotel, The, 163

Old Crow, The, 79

Old Jail Museum, 67

Original People's Temple, The, 179

Oscar, the Beast of 'Busco, 8

Oz Museum, The (Yellow Brick Road Gift Shop), 7

Park on the Sidewalk, Walk in the Street, 12

Philo T. Farnsworth TV Museum, 20

Pizza King, 87

Rainforest Car Wash, 89

Real Hoosiers, The, 91

Real Quayle Trail, The, 28

Remains of the World's First Ferris Wheel, 9

Remnants of the World's Largest Deciduous Tree, 165

Rock House Inn, 143

RV/MH Heritage Foundation/Hall of Fame, 15

Ryan White, Pariah, 83

Ryan White's Real Hometown and Grave, 65

Santa Claus Town, 153

Shoe Tree, 141

Sleep in a Train (Crowne Plaza Union Station), 181

Speedway and the Hall of Fame Museum, The, 189

Spiritualist Camp (Camp Chesterfield), 69

Square Donuts, 100

Squire Boone Caverns and Village, 133

Stiffy Green, the Stiff Dog (Highland Cemetery, Vigo County Museum), 101

Stone Head, 157

Studebaker National Museum and Archives, The, 48

Submarine Superstar (Lighthouse Museum), 4

Thou Shall Not Steal (Shrine of Our Lady of Consolation), 136

Tippecanoe Battlefield Monument, 60

Touchables Sculpture Garden, The, 139

Towns Torn in Half, 104

Tree on the Courthouse, 80

Trigger-Happy Warship, 162

USS *Indianapolis* Memorial, 182

Virgil I. Grissom State Memorial (Spring Mill State Park), 142

Where the Gipper Croaked (Notre Dame/Washington Hall), 49

William Arnold, Truck Stop Artist, 81

Wolf Park, 61

World's Fattest Man Death Site, 4

World's First Automobile (Elwood Haynes Museum), 84

World's First Pay Toilets, 103

World's First Traffic Light (Carmel-Clay Historical Society), 187

World's Largest Egg, 38

World's Largest Living Sign (Bendix Woods), 42

World's Largest Steer, 86

World's Largest Sycamore Stump, 86

World's Largest Trowel, 183

World's Second Largest Clock, 124

Wrenching Barn, A, 62

Wyandotte Cave, 134

Yenawine Exhibit (Carnegie Center for Art and History), 145